■SCHOLASTIC

The Substitute Teacher RESOURCE BOOK

GRADES 3–5

by Mary Rose

NEW YORK • TORONTO • LONDON • AUCKLAND • SYDNEY
MEXICO CITY • NEW DELHI • HONG KONG • BUENOS AIRES

Teaching
Resources

ROCKFORD PUBLIC LIBRARY

To Dot Hanson, MaryAnn Kantu, Susie McGraw, Nell Rogers, Connie Wadsworth, and all the other great substitute teachers it has been my pleasure to know. Thanks for doing a great job in my classroom and in the many classrooms you serve.

Credits: Activities reprinted with permission: pages 70 and 71 "The Case of the Frog Prince" and "The Case of the Terrible Tooth Fairy" from *Grammar Cop* ©Scholastic, 2004; page 72 "The Animal Thieves" from *Storyworks* © Scholastic, 2002; pages 74–75 "The Wonderful Pied Piper," adapted from *Baldwin's Readers* © American Book Company, 1897; pages 76–79 "The Blue Carbuncle," adapted from the short story by Sir Arthur Conan Doyle; pages 88–89 "Whales & Dolphins" from Ready-to-Go Reproducibles: 24 Nonfiction Passages for Test Practice (Scholastic, 2002) © Michael Priestly; page 90 "Get the Picture" from Scholastic Super Science Blue © Scholastic, 1995.

Scholastic Inc. grants teachers permission to photocopy the reproducibles from this book for classroom use. No other part of this publication may be reproduced in whole or in part, or stored in a retrieval system, or transmitted in any form or by any means, electronic, mechanical, photocopying, recording, or otherwise, without permission of the publisher. For information regarding permission, write to Scholastic Teaching Resources, 557 Broadway, New York, NY 10012-3999.

Cover design by Maria Lilja
Cover art by Neografika
Interior design by Melinda Belter
Interior illustrations by Melinda Belter (pages 32, 43, 75, 79, and 83), Jack Deroscher (pages 70 and 71), Greg Harris (page 88), and Mike Moran (pages 24, 47, 62, 63, 67, 68, 72, 76, and 81–83)

Copyright © 2005 by Mary Rose. All rights reserved.
ISBN 0-439-44411-X
Printed in the U.S.A.

2 3 4 5 6 7 8 9 10   40   13 12 11 10 09 08 07 06 05

CONTENTS

INTRODUCTION FOR THE CLASSROOM TEACHER

———————————●———————————

Dear Classroom Teachers,

You may know that for several years I wrote a column in *Instructor* magazine entitled "Ask Mary." It was a "Dear Abby" format in which teachers would ask me questions and I would answer them in the column. One day I got this question from a substitute teacher:

> Dear Mary,
>
> Why do classroom teachers treat substitute teachers so badly? We really feel like second-class citizens, but we perform a valuable service for teachers and for students.

When I read this, I instantly felt a tinge of guilt—not because I have treated my substitutes badly, but because they have been overlooked and underappreciated by our whole profession. So this book is for them, but it is also for you—the regular teacher. Together we can make the job of the substitute teacher easier and in doing so, help him or her be much more effective in our classrooms.

Giving your substitute clear directions and the needed tools will make his or her day go more smoothly, will offer you peace of mind while you are absent, and most importantly, will ensure that your students remain productive while you are gone. But you can do more. Very simply, you can offer the substitute a measure of the respect that they deserve.

This is the answer that I wrote for the "Ask Mary" column:

Dear Substitute,

You are correct that substitute teachers have not garnered the respect they deserve. Teachers who have spent their careers in their own classrooms often do not have an appreciation for the difficulties you face every day. So this letter is for all "regular" teachers out there. Please take a moment for some random acts of kindness for these hardworking professionals.

• When you know there is a sub, step into his or her classroom, introduce yourself, and say, "Welcome to our school."

• Offer to take any students who are disruptive and to make copies or provide worksheets that might be helpful.

• See if he or she knows where the adult restrooms are and offer to buy some coffee.

• Offer to answer questions about the daily schedule, and give directions about where to send students for classes such as speech and music.

• At lunchtime, save the sub a seat beside you and after lunch make sure he or she is on time to pick up students.

• After school, thank the sub for being at your school and for doing a great job.

Thanks for all you do for students! —Mary

It is my hope that this book will help you prepare for the substitute and will allow you to work with this person for the best use of instructional time for your students.

Planning in Advance for an Absence . . . You'll Be Glad You Did

Few of the absences you call in will be emergencies—more likely you'll know in advance that you'll need a substitute for a professional development day or a doctor's appointment—and knowing in advance gives you time to develop an effective plan for your substitute and students. As you plan for your absence, think through your substitute's day and try to lay things out in the order in which they will be used. Picture your morning routine and how you automatically reach for lunch count forms and the attendance folder. Then think of the order of subjects that he or she will be expected to teach that day. Leave specific instructions about what the students should and should not do, such as, "Use crayons or colored pencils to complete the graph, no markers please." Let the substitute know where you keep supplies in case a student does not have his or her own.

TIP

Keep handy in your personal organizer or address book your district's substitute center phone number and the names and substitute ID numbers of preferred substitutes.

TIP

Show one or two responsible students where you keep your materials for the substitute.

TIP

Contact another teacher at your school and ask him or her to check on the substitute for you. In cases of major or unexpected emergencies, ask this trusted colleague to explain your absence to the students.

Use the checklist on page 6 to help you prepare materials and outline essential procedures. Many of these items should not require much effort on your part, because they may be used on a daily basis. Some items are just for emergencies and a few are essential to make the day go well for both the substitute and for your students.

Substitute-Ready Classroom Checklist

❑ **Class schedule** (reproducible page 9) Make a schedule for the day or week that includes times for announcements, lunch, recess, special classes such as art and music, and so on. If you have this posted in your classroom already, simply let the substitute know where it is. Also include:

○ **Clear and complete directions for the day**, listing times that different subjects should be taught, giving directions that explain who does what and when, and telling where to find materials such as answer guides or teacher's editions.

○ **A schedule for students with special needs** who will be leaving the room for assistance or receiving help from an aide.

○ **A medication schedule**, which shows the time and place to send the student for medication. You might highlight this important information in a bright color.

Note: If you're using the reproducible on page 9, fill in only the general schedule at the beginning of the year and keep copies on hand to fill in with specific details for each day you are absent.

❑ **Class list** Provide the first and last names of your homeroom students as well as names of students who may enter your room as they change classes for any subject. You can adapt the Multipurpose Chart on page 16 to create a class list with categories that the substitute can check off for great behavior, work turned in, and so on.

❑ **Seating chart** Be sure to include seating charts for your homeroom and for other classes if students change classes.

❑ **Name tags** These are especially helpful if students do not wear school name tags or if their names are not on desktop stickers. Students can make a stand-up tag out of construction paper or you can provide stick-on name tags. Write these out ahead of time if you can.

❑ **Daily procedures** (reproducible page 10) Explain how you expect the substitute to do the following:

○ **Attendance** Give the location of the folder and specific instructions as to how to fill it out.

○ **Restroom breaks**

○ **Recess**

○ **Lunch** Give the location of the lunch count materials and specific instructions as to how to proceed.

○ **Dismissal**

❑ **Dismissal procedures and bus information** (reproducible page 11) Let the substitute know who walks, rides a bike, rides in a car, goes to day care or after-school care, and who rides which bus. If you are responsible for taking students to their various destinations after school, include directions for the substitute to do so.

❑ **Class rules and discipline procedures** (reproducible page 13) Explain your management system in detail. The substitute should know what rewards and consequences are appropriate and, if necessary, how to assign points or rewards for behavior.

❑ **Emergency procedures and other helpful information**
(reproducible page 12) Be sure to include information about the following:

○ **Directions for fire and tornado drills**
Directions for these emergencies should be posted in your classroom. Be sure to have your own practice drills near the beginning of school so that students do not have to depend on a substitute teacher to give them instructions.

○ **Names of reliable students** Let the substitute know which students to call on for help with finding things, bringing materials to the office, and so on.

○ **Name and location of a buddy teacher**
Leave the name of a nearby colleague for the substitute to check in with if he or she has questions or concerns. (Make sure the buddy teacher knows that you have left his or her name as a helper.)

○ **Groupings throughout the day**
Make sure the substitute has updated lists of students who change classes for reading, math, and any other subjects.

❑ **Personal note to students** On the chalkboard or chart paper, write a positive note outlining your expectations to the class. Hang it up after the students have left so they will see it the next morning. Remind them that you will return soon. Include your signature at the bottom. For example,

Good morning, class! I just found out I have to be absent today. I am sorry that I couldn't let you know ahead of time, but I know you will make the best of this day. Please be helpful and kind to the substitute. Thanks for working hard and cooperating to make this day go smoothly. I can't wait to see a great report when I return.

❑ **Helper chart** If you assign jobs for specific students, let the sub know where to find that information.

❑ **Map of the school showing the classroom location** This is available through your school office and is usually posted in your room for fire drill purposes. Make sure the substitute can find it easily.

❑ **Extras** Always leave a few math pages, word games, or brainteasers that the substitute can use if he or she runs out of things to do. If you are reading a chapter book to the class, ask the substitute to continue reading. Leave math or reading flash cards so the substitute can play a quick game and help the students review skills. Keep these "extras" in a box, folder, or drawer clearly marked "SUBSTITUTE." (See page 27 for more on creating a substitute box.)

❑ **Computer information** Do you want students to use computers in your absence? Make your wishes clear and leave detailed instructions if students will be using the computers independently. Do not expect the substitute to be computer-savvy.

❑ **Rules for the playground**
Many schools have more than one playground and specific times that students are allowed to go there. Make this clear to your substitute so there is no doubt about these rules.

❑ **Substitute report form**
(reproducible page 15) Encourage the substitute to fill out the reproducible feedback form on page 30 to help you plan for your next absence. Be aware that your school may require the substitute to complete a standard form when the day is complete. If that is a requirement, place a copy with the materials for the day.

Tips for Creating a Substitute Folder

Many schools require the classroom teacher to complete a substitute folder that stays on file in the school office. This folder is given to the substitute when he or she arrives. Many of the items listed on previous pages may be included in that folder along with discipline referral forms and a few easy activity papers. See fill-in reproducible forms for creating your own substitute folder on pages 9–15.

To create your own substitute folder, select a folder or binder that has pockets. Then copy and complete the following charts and place them all in the folder. In the pockets, you can put extra lunch-count, attendance, and discipline referral forms and a copy of Discipline Dos and Don'ts, pages 45–48. This way, you can be sure that your substitute will have these essentials without having to look on your desk for them.

Consider purchasing tabs and dividers for the folder. Separate the materials into "student information," "schedules and procedures," "emergency information," and "extra activities."

Ask the office to give this to the person who will be your substitute. Be sure to note in your plans for the substitute to return this folder to the office or to leave it on your desk for you when you return.

TIP

Want to be especially nice? Here are a few little things you can do to let your substitutes know how much you appreciate the difficult job that they do:

- Pay for their morning coffee or tea ahead of time.
- Leave stickers or small rewards for them to distribute to students.
- Clean your desk and chalkboard so they start out in a pleasant environment.
- Include name tags for all students.
- Leave a note saying thanks or saying they do not have to grade the papers.
- Ask them what you could have done to make their job easier.
- Buy them a copy of this book!

SUBSTITUTE FOLDER FORMS

Weekly Schedule

Remember to include times for announcements, recess, restroom breaks, and so on. Use a highlighter to call attention to important details.

Time	Monday	Tuesday	Wednesday	Thursday	Friday

Special Notes About Today's Schedule

Schedule for Students With Special Needs

Name	Needs/Services	Time	Teacher/Room

Medication Schedule

Name	Time	Nurse/Room

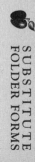

Daily Procedures

This is the way we handle…

Attendance

_____

_____

_____

Location of attendance folder: _____

_____

Lunch count

_____

_____

_____

Location of lunch cards or tickets: _____

_____

_____

Recess

_____

_____

_____

After school

_____

_____

_____

_____

Hallways

_____

_____

_____

Restroom

_____

_____

_____

_____

Lunch

_____

_____

_____

Dismissal

_____

_____

_____

(See page 11 for a list of students who ride the bus, walk, or are picked up)

Dismissal Time _____

Students Who Ride the Bus

Bus _____

_____
_____
_____
_____

Bus _____

_____
_____
_____
_____

Bus _____

_____
_____
_____
_____

Bus _____

_____
_____
_____
_____

Bus _____

_____
_____
_____

Bus _____

_____
_____
_____

Bus _____

_____
_____
_____

Bus _____

_____
_____
_____

Students Who Walk

_____
_____
_____
_____

_____
_____
_____
_____

Students Who Are Picked Up

_____
_____
_____

_____
_____
_____

Other Notes About After-School Care

_____
_____
_____
_____

People Who Can Help

Reliable Students

_____

_____

_____

Buddy Teacher

_____

Room   *Phone Number*

_____   _____

School Office Number

_____

Principal's Name

_____

Emergency Procedures

Fire Drill

_____

_____

_____

_____

_____

_____

Weather Disaster

_____

_____

_____

_____

_____

_____

_____

Special Groupings Throughout the Day

_____ _____ _____ _____

_____ _____ _____ _____

_____ _____ _____ _____

_____ _____ _____ _____

Group   **Purpose**   **Time**

_____   _____   _____

_____   _____   _____

_____   _____   _____

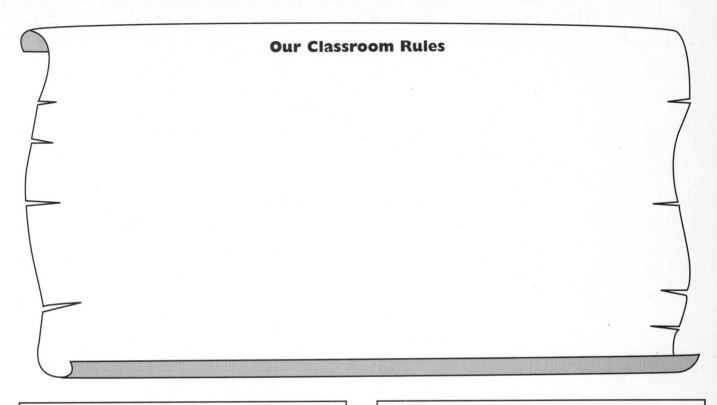

Our Classroom Rules

☆☆ Rewards ☆☆

*When students follow the rules
and are cooperative & productive…*

XX Consequences XX

When students break the rules…

Multipurpose Chart

Name

Substitute Teacher Feedback Form

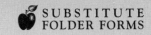

Date _____

Class _____

Name of Substitute Teacher _____

Phone/E-mail _____

	Inadequate/Frustrating	. . . .	Great/Successful
Overall, my day with your class was	1 2	3	4
The lesson plans I found were	1 2	3	4
Our ability to stick to today's schedule was	1 2	3	4
Student behavior and time spent on task was	1 2	3	4

Students who helped _____

_____

Students who worked well _____

_____

Students who had trouble today _____

_____

Student Name   **Action Taken**

_____

_____

_____

Suggestions and Comments

_____

_____

_____

_____

Easy Projects You Can Prepare in Advance of Your Absence

If you know you are going to be absent, set up the substitute day (or days) by starting a couple of projects ahead of time. A little advance planning can ensure that the time students spend with a substitute is not just full of busywork but is organized to contribute to the yearlong goals that you have for their learning. Here are some suggestions to follow if you have the luxury of knowing ahead of time that you will be out of the classroom. All of them will leave the substitute with meaningful, quiet, structured activities to present to your students.

TIP

As a general rule, if a substitute is assigned for one or two days, he or she should not be required to <u>teach</u> any new material. Substitutes may introduce vocabulary for a reading activity, for example, but everything else you leave should be practice on previously covered material.

Writing: "My School's the Best" —A Step-by-Step Essay

If your students are working on written expression practice, have them complete the graphic organizer on page 18 and the first paragraph on a day you are there. When you are gone the next day, the directions to the substitute will be to assist students in finishing their writing and proofreading the paper. The following day the directions to the substitute will be to allow students to illustrate their completed essays. If there is a third (and fourth) day, the substitute can allow students to read their essays out loud to the class and show the illustrations. (Pages 17–20 provide a detailed description of this activity.)

Activity adapted from *10 Easy Writing Lessons That Get Kids Ready for Writing Assessments* by Mary Rose (Scholastic, 1999).

Preparation time: 1–2 writing periods, depending on students' abilities.

Getting started: Have students explain why theirs is a good school. Write this prompt on the chalkboard or chart paper:

> Most kids think that their own school is a great place to spend the day.
>
> What do you like about your school?
>
> Write an essay to explain why your school is great.

First: **Discuss the prompt.** On the chalkboard or chart paper, list several things that students like about their school. Let students generate this list, which might include such topics as nice teachers, great science classes, well-stocked library, big playground, lots of assemblies, good lunches, active PE classes, frequent parties, interesting textbooks, fair principal, and so on.

Second: **Create a model graphic organizer.** On a large sheet of chart paper or the chalkboard, draw a horizontal and vertical line through the center, so that the paper or space is divided in quarters. Have students take out two sheets of paper and do the same thing on their first sheet. On your model, leave the top left corner box empty and in each of the other three spaces, list one thing that *you* like about the school, such as *great kids, active PTA*, and *effective principal*. Have students leave the first box (top left hand) on their papers empty, and in each of the remaining boxes have them select from the list the three things that they like most about the school and write one in each space.

Next, demonstrate how to write one or two details in each of these three boxes that explains why you chose that topic. See the organizer example on page 18.

TIP

Some kids might not think their school is "a great place to spend the day." Don't let those kids with negative suggestions take over the discussion. Remind them to focus on what is good about school instead of what they don't like. Use some humor to diffuse any negativity, and make your own suggestions about positive aspects of the school and begin your own model. (Or invite them to use their criticisms in an editorial piece written to the principal outlining suggestions for change.)

CENTERVILLE TIGERS	GREAT KIDS
orange and black; Mr. Rowe, principal	they work hard, have a sense of humor, and complete their homework
EFFECTIVE PRINCIPAL	ACTIVE PTA
short meetings, hires good teachers, and is fair about discipline	enjoyable fund-raisers, helpful to the teachers, and provide good parties for students

After your demonstration, students should look at their own three topics and write a couple of supporting details under each topic. Make suggestions to individual students and continue the discussion about your good school. Now these students have completed a graphic organizer plan of what they are going to write.

In the empty box, write the name of the school mascot, the school colors, and either the teacher's name or the principal's name. Following this graphic organizer, students will learn how to "write in a circle" to create an introduction and a closing.

Third: Create an introduction. Instruct students to write a traditional heading at the top of the second sheet of paper. You do the same on a sheet of chart paper or the chalkboard. Let the students help you create a universal introduction. Look at the first box on the graphic organizer that contains the mascot name. Use this, plus the names of people at school, to create a universal introduction—this means that *every* student will write the *same* words for their introduction and they will copy it from your model. Here are two examples that the teacher could use with only a few changes:

ROAR!!!!! That is the sound of the Centerville Tigers! We roar because this is the best school in Jackson County! The great kids and Mr. Rowe, our principal, make it a special place to come each day.

Splash! You have just been greeted by the Centerville Dolphins. They are the mascot for the best school in Jackson County. "Welcome to our school," says our principal, Mrs. Smith.

If necessary, write only one or two words at a time so students can keep up with you. Wait for all students to copy the introduction onto their papers. Now students are ready to begin their own writing. Remember that this is an expository essay, meaning that students are to give reasons why something is true.

Fourth: **Begin the body of the essay.** Do your model first. Start a new paragraph under the introduction. *You* write: I think _____ is a great school because of _____. (From the example above you would write: *I think Centerville Elementary is a great school because of the terrific kids.*) Students will write the same sentence, inserting their school's name and a first reason taken from their own graphic organizer. All of the essays in the room will be focused on the same topic sentence, but all will highlight different reasons why students like their school. For example, *I think Centerville is a great school because of the great PE classes.*

Fifth: **Add supporting details.** Continuing to model, you would then write two things about those great kids. *(Students at Centerville Elementary are kind and helpful to each other. They work hard to finish their assignments.)* Then students will need to write two sentences to support their own reason for liking their school. Allow several students to read their essays-in-progress out loud and let students discuss how each detail supported or could be revised to support the reason given.

Sixth: **Prepare for your absence.** At this point you can have students stop work. Collect the started essays and graphic organizers and place them in a folder, a piece of folded construction paper or an envelope. Leave the work for the substitute to take up in your absence. Let students know that they will continue to write their essays while you are gone. Give clear directions about writing two more paragraphs with reasons why they like the school.

Leave your examples and the following directions for the substitute:

INSTRUCTIONS FOR A 1-DAY ABSENCE

Yesterday my students began writing an expository essay, "My School's the Best." Distribute their graphic organizers and first paragraphs and allow them a few minutes to reread what they have already written. Then write the sentence below on the board introducing the second paragraph and have students copy and complete it using an idea from their own graphic organizer: **Another reason Centerville is great is the _____ .** Students should then write at least two supporting sentences to explain this second reason.

When most of the class has completed this, write the following sentence on the board introducing the third paragraph and have students copy and complete it using the last idea from their graphic organizer: **Centerville Elementary also has great _____ .** Students should then write at least two supporting sentences to explain this third reason.

Please collect the essays and graphic organizers at the end of the writing session. Thank you!

If you are going to be absent two or three days, leave the following directions in addition to the directions for day one:

CONTINUED INSTRUCTIONS FOR A TWO-TO-THREE-DAY ABSENCE

Day two: Distribute the essays and organizers. Have students reread what they have written and make any corrections or additions that are necessary. Select a student to read the introduction out loud. Then work as a class to create a two- or three-sentence concluding paragraph that mentions the sound you began with (i.e., "roar!" or "splash!"), the name of the school, the name of the principal or the name of the teacher. This is called "writing in a circle." It simply means that something from the introduction is used in the closing. This makes the essay seem whole and complete—one of many things scorers are looking for in state writing assessments. Example closings for this essay:

—Centerville Elementary is a roaring wonderful school. Come visit us and see for yourself.

—Now you know why Mrs. Smith is proud of the Centerville Dolphins. Ours is the best school around!

If time allows after students have completed the closing, ask students to create an illustration of some favorite aspect of their school that they wrote about. Have them draw on construction paper and staple their completed essays to it, using it as a cover. I will display the essays on a bulletin board when I return.

If there is a third or fourth day of absence, instruct the substitute to allow students to continue their illustrations and to read the completed essays out loud in small groups or to the class.

TIP

You can make the substitute's job even easier by writing model sentences for the class to complete on chart paper. Have the substitute hang up your model to which you have added these two topic sentences:

—Another reason Centerville Elementary is great is the _____ .

—Centerville Elementary has great _____ .

Be sure to leave a large space after the first sentence.

Use a marker with a different color to write students a short note about how to continue work on their essays. Your signature on the note lets students know that you have carefully planned this assignment, and that you are expecting it to be completed. This will help the substitute establish credibility and will help your students to continue their good-quality work in your absence.

Reading: End-of-Book Review

Completely read and discuss a story from the reading basal or plan to end a novel the day before you are going to be absent. Write comprehension questions from the story on a piece of chart paper and review them with students. Discuss what kinds of answers you expect them to create. The following day the substitute can simply hang up the questions and students can go right to work.

Comprehension Questions to Fit Any Book

1. What is the setting of the story?
   How do you know that is the setting?

2. What words would you use to describe the main character? Why did you choose those particular words?

3. What is the main idea of the story or article? Can you explain it to me using only three sentences?

4. Does the author offer an opinion? What is it? Do you agree?

5. Does the author try to teach you a lesson? What lesson?

6. How did the author try to make his or her story or article come alive? Can you find examples of similes or strong verbs or great description?

Reading: Read-Aloud Plays

The day before you are going to be absent, introduce a play, discuss the setting, and assign parts for the students. Have them read and study their parts as homework. Leave a copy with students' names written by their parts and give the substitute directions to allow students to read the play out loud in class. (See pages 76–79 for a read-aloud mystery play and page 56 for teaching tips to help the substitute.) Other read-aloud plays can match your social studies units, for example Scholastic's *Read-Aloud Plays* series includes these topics: Explorers, Medieval Times, Colonial America, Revolutionary War, Pioneers, Immigration, Civil War, World War II, and Civil Rights.

A Tasty Follow-Up:
Science and Math Activities

Many science and math projects require students to complete an activity or experiment on one or two days and then complete a graph or write a response to what they have learned the second day. If you do the hands-on part of the activity the days you are there, you can leave the follow-up graphing or responding for the substitute. The following activity involves sorting and representing parts of a whole as fractions, using colored candies.

The day before you are going to be absent, provide each student with an individual package of 10 to 15 small candies such as M&Ms or Skittles. (You can save money by purchasing a large bag and scooping them into sandwich-size self-sealing bags, one bag for each student. Use a permanent marker to write student names on the bags so there is no argument about whose candy is whose. Using the self-sealing bags is a good idea if the students want to take their candy home, but remind them that there is no eating allowed in the halls or on the school bus!) Distribute copies of page 24 and review the directions with students. Then have students complete the data sheet. Check students' calculations and collect the sheets. Leave them for the substitute teacher along with centimeter graph paper and copies of page 25 (the graphing directions and follow-up questions).

TIP

If you do not want to give students candy, the same activity can be done using any small colored counters such as Unifix cubes.

TIP

You might draw on a piece of chart paper the graph template on page 25 so that the substitute can simply hang it up and review the directions. Your signature at the bottom of the chart lets students know that the assignment is genuine and encourages them to continue their quality work in your absence.

INSTRUCTIONS TO THE SUBSTITUTE

On the enclosed Count 'Em Up! Data Sheets students have recorded the numbers of colored candies they received yesterday. Distribute these data sheets along with the graph paper and the direction sheets to each student. Hang up the sample data provided on chart paper (or draw the data chart shown below on the chalkboard). Tell students that they will create a graph showing the number of colored candies that they had in their bags yesterday. Use chart paper (or the chalkboard) to model step-by-step for students to complete the assignment.

Count 'Em Up Data Sheet

Name Mary

Sorting Your Candies and Recording Your Data

1. Write the names of colors of the candies in your bag. in a bag of this type of candy, even if you don't have a your classmates' bags to be certain you haven't missed

2. Now open your bag and arrange the pieces by colors. number that tells how many of each color you have. (color in your bag.) These numbers are called *whole nu*

3. Count how many candies you have in all and write th *total.*

4. Tell more about the candies using fractions, or parts o number of a fraction (denominator) tells how many p The top number (numerator) tells how many pieces yo Look at the example. It shows 4 red candies out of a t Now use fractions to write the part of the total numbe on your chart. Each time, the denominator showing th be the same.

5. Write the number that tells how many of each color you have.

	Colors	Numbers	Fractions	Total Candies
Example:	red	4	4/13	13
	blue	3	3/17	3
	brown	4	5/17	5
	yellow	5	4/17	4
	red	2	2/17	2
	green	3	3/17	3
TOTAL		17		

Add all of the numerals in the "numbers" column. This number and the total number you counted should be the same. If they are not, count your colors and your candies again.

24

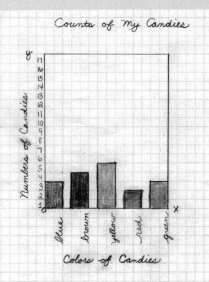

Counts of My Candies

Numbers of Candies

Colors of Candies

TIP

Less experienced students will have difficulty following these directions. To make it easier, the substitute can create his or her own graph using imaginary numbers of candies. The students will make their graph like the substitute's model using their own data.

The steps to creating a graph are described on page 24.

Count 'Em Up! Data Sheet

Name _____ Date _____

Sorting Your Candies and Recording Your Data:

1. Write the names of the colors of the candies in your bag. Write every color you might find in a bag of this type of candy, even if you don't have any of those in your bag. (Look at your classmates' bags to be certain you haven't missed any colors.)

2. Now open your bag and arrange the pieces by colors. Beside the color name, write the number that tells how many of each color you have. (Use a zero if you do not have that color in your bag.) These numbers are called *whole numbers*.

3. Count how many candies you have in all and write that number in the space marked *total*.

4. Tell more about the candies using fractions, or parts of whole numbers. The bottom number of a fraction (denominator) tells how many pieces there are altogether. The top number (numerator) tells how many pieces you are talking about at that time. Look at the example. It shows four red candies out of a total of 13 candies altogether. Now use fractions to write the part of the total number of candies shown by each color on your chart. The denominator showing the total number of candies will be the same each time.

5. Write the number that tells how many of each color you have.

Colors	Numbers	Fractions	Total Candies
Example: red	4	$^4/_{13}$	13
_____	_____	_____	_____
_____	_____	_____	_____
_____	_____	_____	_____
_____	_____	_____	_____
_____	_____	_____	_____
_____	_____	_____	_____
_____	_____	_____	_____
_____	_____	_____	_____
TOTAL	_____		

Add all of the numerals in the "numbers" column. This number and the total number you counted should be the same. If they are not, count your colors and your candies again.

The Substitute Teacher Resource Book • Scholastic Teaching Resources

Count 'Em Up! Graphing

Name _____ Date _____

Making Your Graph:

Title _____

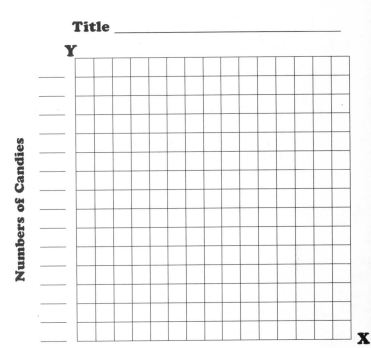

1. Draw and label the X-axis at the bottom of your graph. Just below the X-axis write the color names of candies from your data sheet. You may have to write sideways to get the word in. Use two squares (2 cm) for each color word.

2. Along the left side of the graph, draw the Y-axis. Turn your paper sideways and write "Numbers of Candies" to label this axis. Where the two axis lines meet, write a zero. Go up the Y-axis of the graph, counting by ones. Write a number by each square.

3. Use your data sheet to fill in the graph. Above each color word, shade in the correct number of squares that will tell how many of that color of candy you had. Use crayons or colored pencils to match the color categories. If you did not have any candy of a particular color, you should leave the spaces above the color blank to show zero.

4. Give your graph a title. Write it at the top of the graph.

Hint: Count the colored squares on your graph. Is this number the same as the total on your data sheet? It should be! Check your graph if it isn't.

5. Answer the following questions about your graph. Turn your papers in when you are finished with these questions.

1. This graph is called a bar graph. What color bar on your graph is the highest? _____

2. What color is the lowest bar? (Be careful! Did you have any amount equal to zero?) _____

3. How many candies would you have if you added the bars showing your greatest two amounts together? _____

4. How many candies would you have if you added the bars showing your least two amounts together? _____

5. How many candies would you have if you added all the colors together? _____

The Substitute Teacher Resource Book • Scholastic Teaching Resources

Worthy Workbook Assignments

Another good practice is to have students tear particular pages out of their workbooks and staple these together. Have them write their names on the top page in the pile. Then go over the directions for each page in the packet. Do one or two questions on the most challenging pages and collect the packets. The following day (or days), the substitute can pass out the work and be assured that the students know what to do.

You can do the same thing in math by creating packets of work for students to complete. The strength of this plan is that students know ahead of time what is expected of them. They will not be able to say that the substitute got confused or they did not know what to do on a certain page. Let students know that you do expect them to finish the work and that it is for a grade—or let them know that there are more pages than they can complete in one or two days and that it is okay if they don't finish but they will have the opportunity to complete it later. This way, you can be sure they will take the assignment seriously.

Give a Test

The day before you are going to be absent, rearrange the students' desks so that they are far apart. Then go over all of the material that will be on an upcoming test. The substitute can administer the test in your absence. It is usually a very quiet activity and if the desks are apart, there is little chance of distractions or cheating. In your plans, remind the substitute to circulate around the room during the test. If you think it is necessary to provide privacy for the students while they work, then leave blank folders that can be set up on each desk to shield papers from other students' eyes.

Do not expect your substitute to give performance assessments or any type of local, state, or standardized test. These usually require training so that they will be properly administered. Check with your principal if you know you will be absent on testing days.

Videos With Purpose

If you opt to have the substitute show a video, follow these guidelines:
- Avoid using the video as an entertainment tool to take up time. Planning in advance will provide engaging materials for students to work on and a useful purpose for your substitute (who is not a babysitter!).
- Make sure the content of the video connects with academic subject matter that you're teaching. Can it be followed up with comprehension questions or a critical response assignment?
- Check whether it is legal to show the video. Be aware that it is illegal to rent a video and show it in your classroom. It is also illegal to tape certain shows from your television at home and show them at school.
- Preview the video. Be certain that the movie is free of explicit language, unnecessary violence, religious proselytizing, and sexual content.
- Select a video from your school library. Choose a science or social studies topic or a movie version of a story your students have read. Use the teacher's guide for a follow-up activity or create a page for students to complete after viewing the information. For example, you might have students use a Venn diagram to compare the differences and similarities of the novel and the film that has been adapted from the novel.

Putting It All Together: The Substitute Box

Long before the need arises—as soon as the year begins, if possible—gather a collection of materials that can be used with a substitute teacher. These should be clearly marked "SUBSTITUTE" and can be stored in an expandable folder, a plastic box, or a file-cabinet drawer. Make sure your colleagues and some of your more reliable students know where you keep these materials. You can add to this collection all year long. Just gather extra activity pages, workbook pages, skill sheets, word games, or even craft ideas connected to concepts or skills you've taught. You may need these things in preparation for your own substitute, or you may share it with a substitute who has been called in on an emergency basis for a colleague. Anyone will be able to go to that box and keep students occupied with quality work. This box, coupled with the items on the checklist on pages 6–7 and a couple of projects from the Easy Projects You Can Prepare in Advance of Your Absence section on pages 16–26 will ensure that your students are well provided for even in an emergency.

Important Follow-Up Tips for When You Return

When you return from your absence, you may choose to record grades for the work completed with the substitute. Whether you record the scores or not, be sure to mark each paper that has been completed, even if you put on only a star or a sticker, and hand them back to students. This will let students know that you take this work seriously and may send the message to work even harder for a substitute the next time.

Respond to any notes the substitute has left you, look for a list of students with great behavior (a WOW! List) on the chalkboard, and compliment students on the amount of work they have completed.

Hopefully your substitute was well prepared, her day went smoothly, and everyone went home happy. If you do get a report of misbehavior, there are some steps you should take.

1. Find out if a discipline referral was completed.

2. Assess how serious the offense really was. Sometimes students will report things as being terrible and out of hand when really they were just loud because the substitute was there and there was no real offense. Other times they will *not* tell you the whole truth for fear of getting in trouble. If it is not a serious event, let it drop.

TIP

No matter what, avoid group punishments. Remember that no matter what the students report, you cannot be absolutely sure what happened in the classroom. It is highly unlikely that **everyone** was misbehaving, so group punishments (and group rewards) are highly unfair.

3. If there was real trouble, allow your principal to handle it.

4. Ask students to brainstorm how the situation could have been avoided. Could you have left more concrete directions? Could they have sought advice from another teacher? Could they have been more kind and helpful? Could they have monitored themselves more effectively? Were they breaking specific school rules? Did they use their best manners?

Preparing for a Long-Term Absence

It is difficult for most teachers to leave their classrooms for extended periods of time. Some careful preparation can make this process easier for you and for your students.

First, be prepared to have another responsible adult in your room and recognize that this person may not teach the same way that you do and will need some personal space and professional respect. Change the message on your school voice mail so that the caller will know that they have reached the person who is your substitute. (A sample message might sound like this: "You have reached the voice mailbox of Mrs. Smith, the current substitute for Mrs. Jones in grade one. Please leave a message.") Put away or take home anything that is really precious to you, so that he or she does not have to be held responsible for your personal possessions. Clear your classroom of clutter to make the substitute's job easier. Clean out your desk, clear off some shelves for him or her to use, and make sure there is space for this person to "move in" and "own" the classroom in your absence.

Second, set some realistic long-term goals that you can expect this person to meet. Look at your yearlong plan and try to gauge what the sub should cover in your absence. You may give specific directions such as, "Complete the reading workbook up to page 56" or "Have children practice writing numerals to 50," or you may just give general directions such as, "Teach this unit on life cycles."

TIP

Some helpful resources that provide structured sequential lessons with reproducible materials or whole-class sets include my book *Week-by-Week Homework for Building Reading Comprehension and Fluency: Grades 3–6* (Scholastic, 2002) and weekly magazines such as *Scholastic News*, which also connect students with current events.

Third, try to have your schedule set up so that it is both flexible for the substitute teacher and, at the same time, rigid enough that your students can follow a predictable pattern with their responsibilities, homework assignments, and so on. You can make this easier by running off weeks of routine lessons such as spelling or read-aloud homework.

You may want to prepare one hands-on seasonal activity that students can complete and take home some time during your absence. Substitutes do not usually have a file cabinet full of clever ideas and may be reluctant to use materials such as construction paper and glitter unless you have left specific instructions to do so.

Put up a new bulletin board just before you leave so that the sub doesn't have to contend with classroom presentation and decoration during the first week or two.

Fourth, prepare your students. If possible, let them meet the substitute and get to know him or her at least one day while you are both there. Establish a way to communicate with the class. This would be very easy through weekly e-mail letters, but you could also drop your class a quick note during your absence. Be careful that your questions and comments concern the welfare of the students; do not give the impression that you are soliciting students' reactions or checking up on the substitute.

Fifth, plan now for your return by visiting the class just before you come back. You can check the progress of the class and begin to plan the units you will teach next. Be sure to thank the substitute with a small gift or at least a nice note saying you appreciated his or her efforts in your absence.

Evaluating the Substitute's Performance

Let your administrators and colleagues know which substitutes you recommend and which may need extra support when they work at your school. Your principal or other administrator may be able to intervene and help prepare a substitute who is consistently unsuccessful. This form provides a record of your evaluation. Keep a copy for your records.

TIP

Remember to evaluate the quality of the substitute's work—his or her ability to teach and follow the plans in your absence. How much work did students complete and how effectively did they do it? Try not to be overly influenced by stories from students. If you need a gauge, ask colleagues about the substitute's ability to control students in the hallway, at lunch, and at recess.

Substitute Evaluation Form

(to be filled out by the teacher)

School _____

Date of absence _____

Name of classroom teacher _____

Name of substitute teacher _____

The substitute teacher:

	NO	SOMEWHAT	YES
• followed directions for academic instruction.	❑	❑	❑
• controlled the students' behavior.	❑	❑	❑
• left the room neat and orderly.	❑	❑	❑
• arrived and departed at appropriate times.	❑	❑	❑
• completed necessary paperwork in the office.	❑	❑	❑
• handled difficult situations without assistance.	❑	❑	❑

Comments

_____

_____

_____

_____

_____

_____

_____

_____

INTRODUCTION FOR THE SUBSTITUTE TEACHER

Welcome to the dynamic world of the classroom teacher.

The job of the substitute teacher is one of the most challenging jobs in education. It is also one of the most overlooked and underappreciated positions in this country. You are expected to enter a classroom full of unfamiliar students, adapt to specific curriculum and schedules, maintain order, and be on time for everything. Sometimes you will need to deal with students who are grieving for an absent teacher. You may be one of a long parade of substitute teachers the students have seen this school year. You may not get a lot of help or respect from the parents or the teachers in the building. You may be called on with the least amount of notice possible. At times it may seem like an impossible task, but with each assignment, you will gain organization and management skills—and confidence. The ideas and guidelines in this section can help you master these skills and make the most of each day in the classroom.

Step One: Before You Set Foot in the Classroom

Invest a couple of dollars in a large tote bag (or invest 25 cents in a paper shopping bag with sturdy handles). Then spend about $5 at your local copy center to buy a package of cheap stick-on name tags and to make some copies of the reproducibles in the back of this book. Select three or four activities and make about 30 copies of each. (Choose a variety of activities—one just for fun, several for reading, one for math, and so on.) You may carry these around for weeks and never use them, but it will be nice to know you have a backup plan if you need something quickly to occupy your charges. If you have a couple of extra dollars, purchase a small package of "good work" stickers. Avoid designs that are seasonal or specific so that you can use them for any grade at any time.

TIP

If you use some of your copies, you may be permitted to make replacements or extras on school copy machines, which are usually in high demand and subject to rules and restrictions. Be sure to ask permission and to copy only to replace what you have used or are planning to use the following day.

Substitute Tote-Bag Checklist

❑ **A copy of this book**
Refer to it for games, read-alouds, or other classroom suggestions.

❑ **Copies of short and easy books that can be read out loud to the class**
(Choose a variety that will be appropriate for different grade levels. Poetry books are great too. See pages 75–76 for an engaging read-aloud folktale.)

❑ **Adhesive name tags**

❑ **"Good work" stickers**

❑ **Copies of activity pages**

❑ **Your lunch**
(Chances are the cafeteria will be serving something you may not want to eat. Bring your own food and a beverage.)

❑ **Your name tag**
(It is probably required that you wear this when you are on school grounds.)

❑ **Two or three business-size envelopes**

❑ **Area maps, directions to, and phone numbers of schools in your district**

❑ **A phone card and some change for emergency calls or a soda after work**

Dress for a Successful School Day

Remember that in the classroom students will instantly respond to the first impression you give them. Your clothing, hairstyle, and makeup should tell them that you are an adult and that you command their respect. This can be the first step in controlling the behavior of these students.

No one expects teachers to dress like they just walked out of Saks Fifth Avenue, but you do need to be aware that this profession is a conservative one and that parents and other teachers can be very critical of your appearance. Be sure that clothes are business-casual style, provide plenty of coverage, and fit comfortably for all the bending, sitting, walking, and reaching you will be doing in the classroom. Remember . . . if you have to ask yourself if it is appropriate, it probably isn't. *Always* err on the conservative side of this issue.

Step Two: Starting the Day Right

Plan to arrive early and check in at the school office. The secretary will either provide you with a map or show you to your classroom for the day. She may hand you a substitute folder that contains valuable school information, discipline referral slips, clinic passes, and so on. Ask what time you can expect students to arrive in your classroom. This will give you an idea of how much preparation time you have.

You already know that students can be hard on a substitute teacher. They do this because their own daily routine with their teacher has been disrupted and they may be uncomfortable with someone unfamiliar in charge. Further, they may think that having a substitute provides a chance to take a day off from learning or following the rules because substitutes are often not familiar with school or class policies and procedures. You can appear strong and in control if you start the morning in a positive way—and that means *not* relying on students to tell you all of the procedural information.

With each assignment, ask yourself the frequently-asked questions on pages 34–36 and make sure you have the answers to them even before you make a plan for your academic day. Although you may not be able to answer all of these before students arrive, this list and the tips provided will help you get your bearings.

TIP

In the morning, introduce yourself to the principal or assistant principal. You may need his or her help later in the day or you may want to ask him or her for a reference.

Super-Start FAQs

Answers to these questions do vary from school to school. Here are some general guidelines to help you make informed decisions or find the right information. Keep track of different policies at different schools by keeping a copy of School Policy Notes for Substitute Teaching Assignments (page 38) in your tote bag and filling out the form during each assignment.

What is my role during students' arrival?

Students may wait for you in the hallway or elsewhere in the building. You need to know if and where you need to pick them up. The bells may signal important times in the morning schedule. Find out what time the bells ring and what they signify.

How should I take attendance and the lunch count? Where does it go?

This is one of the most important functions you will do all day. Get it right! Ask the secretary or another teacher to explain how to do this. Students are often assigned to deliver this information to the office for you. Find out who the class "runner" is.

How do I start the school day?

Many schools now have intercom announcements or closed-circuit television announcements. This may include playing the National Anthem and repeating the Pledge of Allegiance. You need to know what to expect and have the students quiet and ready for this. Set a good example by standing quietly for the patriotic observances and listening to the announcements.

What should I do with notes and money and forms that students bring from home?

Students often enter the classroom clutching any number of papers and envelopes containing money. Glance at the notes to see if any of them require immediate action from you or tell you that someone is leaving early or going home a different way. Some schools require these parent notes to go to the office. If not, then be sure to put them in a prominent place so that you remember what to do. Put all official school forms and money in one of the large envelopes from your tote bag, write the classroom teacher's name on the outside, and leave it in a secure place for the teacher or take it to the office when you have a break.

Can I assign students jobs or should I follow the "helper chart"?

The helper chart is a big deal to students. If the teacher has assigned someone to take the attendance and lunch forms to the office or be the line leader, it is very important that you call on those students to continue their jobs instead of randomly choosing someone else. Look around the room to see if helper jobs are posted somewhere and use those names. Being prepared to call on the right helper is one more way that you can give the impression of being a person in charge.

Super-Start FAQs continued

Where will my students go? What times will they leave and return?

It is unlikely that you will have those 24 students in your care the entire day. There should be a schedule of who goes where and when. Check the schedule left by the teacher or ask another teacher to see if your students will leave the classroom for exceptional education or speech or other classes. Many elementary schools even change classes for reading and math, which means you may work with a new group of students for part of the school day—one more reason to have a stock of those stick-on name tags!

Make sure you know when and where to go for lunch or for special classes like music, art, or physical education.

You may want to write all of these times on the chalkboard or on a piece of paper so that you can refer to it during the day. Students will instantly feel reassured that you are a person who has everything under control.

Do students have names on their desks or name tags to wear as identification?

If you can call a student by name it will help to establish the feeling that you are someone who cares about students in your charge. It can also help with discipline; when students are sure you know their names, they also realize that they are more likely to be held responsible for their behavior. If there is no way for you to know students' names, plan to use your stick-on name tags from your tote bag in one of the following ways:

1. Look in the class roll or attendance book and quickly print the name of each student on a name tag. Pass the name tags out after the morning announcements and ask students to wear them until you learn their names.

2. Put a blank name tag on each desk and ask students to print their names on the tags and stick them on their clothing.

3. Hold the name tags and a marker in your hand. As you call the roll for attendance, print a name on each card and have each student come to you and receive a name tag. As each student gets a tag, say something to each one: "Good morning," "It's nice to see you today," "I'm happy to meet you," "That is a great shirt," "I like the way you have your hair braided," and so forth.

Not only will you have recognized each student individually, but you have started to learn their names and you have begun your day—and theirs—on a positive note.

How do I manage students' use of the restroom?

To maintain control of the students in your charge, you will need to be cognizant of their whereabouts and behavior even when they leave the classroom. A good rule of thumb is to allow only two students at a time to leave the room for restroom breaks. Even if you have only been with the class a short time, you can probably tell which two should not be out of the room together!

See if the teacher has a policy posted somewhere or if there are restroom passes that students take with them when they leave the room. Ask a nearby teacher about restroom policies. (Do all students go at a designated time of day? Do they go as they change classes from reading or math? How many students are usually allowed in the restroom at a time?) Once again, you want to know the answers before you have to ask any of them.

Super-Start FAQs continued

How do I complete a discipline referral form?

You should complete formal paperwork for any negative behavior that has required more than one verbal reprimand from you or any behavior that has affected the safety of students, the stability of the learning environment, or the physical facilities where students are located. Any time there is negative physical contact between students or gross disrespect shown to you or another child, you should complete a discipline referral for that student.

The policy on discipline referrals varies greatly from district to district. After the usual questions that identify the students involved, there will be spaces for you and for any witnesses to make statements about the events. It is vitally important that you are constantly watching and listening to the students in your control—hence the rules about restrooms! You want to be able to give a clear and accurate account of what transpired. You do not usually name names of other students involved in the altercation. For example, if Mike was pushing Jack, you simply say that Mike pushed another student.

Complete the form, even if you feel the offense may not warrant any action from the principal. The principal can decide the severity of the offense and this will cover you in case there is any legal question about what happened.

What is my role in the dismissal procedure?

You probably have several hours to worry about this, but it is another critically important procedure for you to do correctly. First, consult your substitute folder and nearby teachers, and then check with students. Find out who rides the bus, who walks home, who goes to after-school care, and who gets picked up by a parent or caretaker. (Filling out a copy of the dismissal procedure form on page 11 can help you keep track of all of this information.) Make sure you know what times to dismiss students and whether you are required to escort them to a certain place. Double-check notes that students have brought to school to be sure they do not indicate a change in after-school plans.

TIP

Be sure to allow about 10 to 15 minutes for cleaning up materials and packing backpacks before the earliest dismissal.

Super-Start FAQs continued

How should I greet the students?

This is where you make that important first impression and it may make your whole day go more easily. Plan to stand at the classroom door and greet students as they enter. Try: "Hi, I'm Mr./Ms./Mrs. _____, and I will be your teacher today. Please enter the room quietly, put your things away, and read the note on the chalkboard." Or, "Hi, I'm Mr./Ms./Mrs. _____, and I will be your teacher today. Please enter the room quietly, put your things away, and complete the paper on your desk." Request that students please hold any money or notes from their parents until after the morning announcements.

Students should enter and hang up backpacks; stow lunch boxes, coats, hats, and so on; and walk to their desks.

What can I expect the classroom teacher to leave for me?

This is a list of what the classroom teacher should have left for you (see also the reproducible substitute folder forms on pages referenced below):

1. A complete schedule for the day, including times for arrival, different subjects, lunch, special classes, recess, and dismissal.
2. Notes about any deviations from the regular schedule, such as school assemblies.
3. A schedule of pull-out programs for students receiving extra support services.
4. Lists of students in instructional groups or students who change classes.
5. Procedures for attendance, lunch, recess, hallways, dismissal, after school, and emergency situations.
6. Notes on classroom rules and behavior expectations, including appropriate consequences and rewards.
7. Attendance, lunch, and discipline-referral forms.
8. A lesson plan for the day.

page 9

page 10

page 11

page 12

page 13

page 15

Class Schedule

Weekly Schedule

Remember to include times to call attention to importa...

Time	Monday

Schedule for Studen...

Name

Daily Procedures

This is the way we handle...

Attendance

Location of attendance folder

Lunch count

Location of lunch cards or tick...

Recess

After school

Dismissal & Bus Information

Dismissal Time _____

Students Who Ride the Bus

Bus _____   Bus _____

Bus _____   Bus _____

Students Who Walk

Students Who Are Picked up

Other Notes About After-School Care

Emergency Procedures & Other Useful Information   🍎 SUBSTITUTE FOLDER FORMS

People Who Can Help

Reliable Students

Buddy Teacher

Room _____   Phone Number _____

School Office Number

Principal's Name

Special Groupings Throughout th...

Group

☆☆ **Rewards** ☆
*When students follow the ...
and are cooperative & produ...*

Class Rules & Discipline Procedures   🍎 SUBSTITUTE FOLDER FORMS

Substitute Teacher Feedback Form   🍎 SUBSTITUTE FOLDER FORMS

Date _____

Class _____

Name of Substitute Teacher _____

Phone/E-mail _____

	Inadequate/Frustrating	....	Great/Successful
Overall, my day with your class was	1 2	3	4
The lesson plans I found were	1 2	3	4
Our ability to stick to today's schedule was	1 2	3	4
Student behavior and time spent on task was	1 2	3	4

Students who helped _____

Students who worked well _____

Students who had trouble today _____

Student Name	Action Taken

Suggestions and Comments

School Policy Notes for Substitute Teaching Assignments

Name of School	Grades Taught	Names of Absent Teachers	Procedure Notes	Comments

The Substitute Teacher Resource Book • Scholastic Teaching Resources

Step Three: Implementing Instructional Plans Effectively

⬤

Read over the material that explains what students are to be working on for the first hour. Read the answers, too. You want to make sure you're familiar with everything that is presented to students—even if the material is unfamiliar to you.

1. Print your name on the chalkboard, title first, and stand confidently in front of the room. In a calm, clear voice say, "I am Mr./Ms./Mrs. _____ and I will be your substitute teacher today [or for several days if you know that]. I know that it is difficult to have your teacher away, but we can have a good day if we cooperate and are polite to each other. We will get right to work after the morning announcements." Or "We will get right to work now that the morning announcements are completed."

2. "Before we start reading [or math or another subject], I would like to know each of your names. I will collect lunch money and notes from your parents when I call you. Please work quietly at your desk or read a book at your desk until you hear your name."

3. Pick up the first order of the day as described in the lesson plans left by the teacher. Stand quietly in front of the room and explain what the students will be doing. For example, "Today you will continue studying biographies by reading about Bill Cosby. You will begin reading his story on page 275 and then answer the questions that are on this sheet of paper." Then tell students where they are to put completed work and what they are to do when they finish (perhaps a fun activity page from your tote bag), and then ask, "Are there any questions about the assignment?"

Similar directions might be given in math: "Today you will continue practice with geometry problems. There are several shapes on this page. You are to find the area and perimeter of each one. Remember to show your work in the space beside each problem. Are there any questions about the assignment?"

Make sure students know where to put completed work and what to do if they are finished.

Avoid the temptation to interrupt if the students are actually working quietly. Circulate around the room to see that everyone is on task. If you find a student who is not on task, whisper something like one of the following: "I see you need some help getting started." "Do you have a specific question?" "Do you know what to do first?" "Can I help you with this first one?" "Did you understand the directions?"

By using this technique (circulating and whispering), you help students who are having trouble without embarrassing them and you let everyone know that you are watching to see who is working and who is not.

4. Before going on to the next subject, be sure to thank students for working quietly and completing what you asked them to do. Let them know that you will give a good report to their regular teacher.

5. Continue to follow the teacher's directions as closely as possible. Staying on a predictable schedule makes students comfortable and can actually help with discipline problems. Use a checkmark or star to indicate things you have completed. Make a note on anything that you had to omit or ran out of time to complete. If there is some down time or you have a few minutes to fill before lunch, try asking some of the trivia questions on pages 58–61 or reading some poems found on pages 67–69.

Even the most experienced teachers can misjudge the amount of time it will take students to complete work or how difficult a specific assignment will be. If you find that the students complete the work too quickly, use the activity pages in your tote bag. If you find that the work is too difficult and students cannot finish, stay on the time schedule he or she has suggested. Collect unfinished work and keep it for the teacher to look at and go on to the next subject. On a sticky note, provide some brief notes on each assignment to let the teacher know what areas of difficulty or success students experienced with the particular assignment. This can help the classroom teacher better address particular skill areas when he or she returns. It also helps him or her create more appropriate future lessons for substitute teachers.

No Plans?
Emergency Lessons and Activities

What if I have to substitute teach in an emergency situation? What do I do if there are no plans at all?

If there has been a dire emergency that has pulled the teacher from the classroom, your first obligation is to calm and reassure the students that they will be taken care of and that the school day will proceed as normal.

If there has been an accident of some kind, do not give out any information except the most basic facts. Begin in the usual way, "My name is Mr./Ms./Mrs. _____ and I will be your substitute while your teacher, _____, is absent today." Then offer little or no information to the class. If the news is particularly bad, the school principal or guidance counselor will come in and present what they want the students to know. It is better for the students to get this information from an adult in the school with whom they have an established relationship.

Suggestions of things you might say include:

"Mrs. _____ had to leave school for a little while."

"Mrs. _____ was involved in an accident but I don't have any details. I am sure she would want us to get a lot of work done in her absence."

"Mrs. _____'s husband is sick and she had to leave. I will let you know if I find out when she will return."

"I don't know very many details. I'm sure your principal will be here soon to tell us what has happened."

Your next order of business is to try to make their school day proceed as normally as possible. Decide whether or not to issue name tags. Check the schedule or plan book to see what the students are supposed to be doing. If that fails, then offer them an activity page from your tote bag. Do *not* read them funny poems or play comical games to cheer them up. If the situation is really serious, that may upset students.

If students cannot stay on task and insist on talking about the emergency event, pass out some blank paper and suggest that they write a letter or paragraph about the event or illustrate their feelings. If you know the teacher is ill and will not return soon, allow them to make him or her "Get Well" or "We Miss You" cards. Do *not* offer your views about the situation. Avoid saying anything with religious overtones or discussing death and dying. School guidance counselors or trained child psychologists will handle these situations.

Making Your Own Plans

In some nonemergency cases you may be asked to step into a classroom where there are no plans left specifically for a substitute. In this case, you should try to follow the teacher's plan book. You will find that teachers often write in abbreviations, which you may not be able to decipher, and make references you may not understand. Don't panic.

Most teachers have a daily schedule posted somewhere in the classroom. Look around for it and determine what students should be doing at this time of day. If there is no schedule posted, look at previous weeks in the plan book and see if the teacher has listed times that each subject is usually taught. If neither of these yields any information, contact another teacher or reach into that well-stocked tote bag for a fun activity that can occupy students while you get your bearings.

Here is an example of what you might tell your students in this situation:

"Hello, my name is Mr./Ms./Mrs. _____ and I will be your substitute teacher for the rest of the day. I expect you to follow my directions and treat me, your classmates, and yourselves with respect. I will do the same. While I organize some work for you to complete, you may enjoy this activity page I brought for you. You are welcome to color it if we have time."

No-Fail Activities

Here is a list of other things you can ask students to do if you cannot find work for them.

1. Ask students to get a library book out of their desk or from the classroom shelf and read quietly.

2. Have students get a social studies or science book from their desks and read something the class has not covered yet this year. Then have them write down five interesting facts that they can tell the rest of the class. Let them read their five facts out loud or post them on the wall or bulletin board. (If one or two kids finish quickly, ask them to illustrate one of the facts.)

3. Challenge students to write a short story using as many of this week's spelling words as they can.

4. Choose a short, engaging book from the teacher's shelf or your tote bag. Pass out drawing paper or have students open to a fresh sheet of notebook paper. Read out loud and while they listen, allow the students to illustrate what you read and share their drawings, if they like, when the reading is finished. Discussing the details and story elements (plot, character, setting, theme) is a good way to reinforce what they heard.

5. Pass out 8 x 12-inch sheets of construction paper. Have students fold this in half to make a card or write a letter to the missing teacher.

TIP

Some students may have reading or writing response journals and they can use the strategies they usually use to add a new entry.

6. Have each student write his or her name vertically down the side of a sheet of paper. Then help students create acrostics by writing words that describe themselves and start with the letters in their names. If time allows, let them create a self-portrait that illustrates the words they have written. Display these on the chalkboard for the returning teacher to see.

Example:

T—terrific, talented, tennis player

O—outstanding, outgoing, outloud

M—marvelous, melodramatic

Variations on the acrostic:

Have the students create a short story, written in such a way that each letter of their name begins a new sentence.

Have the students write complete sentences about themselves, written so that each letter of their name begins a new sentence.

Have students write the entire alphabet along the left-hand side of a sheet of paper and try to write words that start with each letter of the alphabet. The words should come from categories such as these:

	SEASONAL WORDS	VERBS	SCHOOL WORDS	SPORTS WORDS
A	autumn	act	arithmetic	athlete
B	bob for apples	burst	books	basketball
C	chrysanthemum	cry	cafeteria	coach

7. Almost all students need to work on making their handwriting more legible. Write a paragraph on chart paper or the chalkboard and instruct students to copy it neatly and precisely. Here are a few guidelines:

- Some early third-grade students may not yet be familiar with cursive writing. In this case, use manuscript instead of cursive.
- If you sense that students can copy in cursive but need extra guidance, write only one or two words at a time and pause while students copy them.
- Use a ruling to show students how to form the letters properly.
- something original, use famous poems or sayings such as —"A penny saved is a penny earned," "When you are best to yourself," and so on.

Management Tips ... Through the Day

...er! The principal and other ... in the classroom, but they will ... students to other subjects, recess, ... one or two extra minutes for ... than late.

...tudents in review work rather than ...ers rarely expect you to introduce new material ...gnment you give will involve skills that students ... not need to review heavily or demonstrate or ... you are in a long-term assignment. ... teacher may ask you to introduce vocabulary ...ce or social studies lesson.

Renew items at: www.rockfordpubliclibrary.org

Customer ID: **********9561

Items that you checked out

Title: The substitute teacher resource book .
Grades K-2
ID: 31112014550335
Due: Wednesday, July 24, 2019

Title: The substitute teacher resource book.
Grades 3-5
ID: 31112014550368
Due: Wednesday, July 24, 2019

Title: Thinking organized for parents and
children : helping kids get organized for
home, school & play
ID: 31112015304542
Due: Wednesday, July 24, 2019

Total items: 3
Account balance: $4.00
7/3/2019 7:05 PM
Checked out: 8
Overdue: 0
Hold requests: 0
Ready for pickup: 0

Thank you for using the Rockford Public
Library

❑ **TIP 3: Phrase your questions wisely.** Notice that a wise substitute asks the class specific questions, such as, "Are there any questions *about the assignment*?" Avoid open-ended questions such as "Are there any questions?", which may invite personal questions that you do not want to answer. If that does happen—and students may ask inappropriate questions, just repeat your question with a caveat, "Are there any questions about the directions on this page?" This will defuse the tension very quickly and make a power struggle with the student less likely.

❑ **TIP 4: Make the start of the day count.** You *may* encounter a school where the morning routine is left up to the classroom teacher, meaning that there are no intercom or television announcements. Check the helper chart to see if someone is assigned to lead a song or the Pledge of Allegiance, or lead this yourself. Remember that classroom teachers always schedule an opening exercise (or exercises) every morning to signify that the school day has officially begun. It is even more important that *you* open with something that sends this message. If all else fails, work with students to plan out the order of subjects or events for the day or read a poem or story with a message about new beginnings or starting the day, such as Dr. Seuss's *Oh, the Places You'll Go!*

❑ **TIP 5: Know the computer use policy.** If you are only going to be in the classroom for one or two days, avoid turning on the computers unless the teacher has left directions to do so. This policy can help you prevent damage to expensive equipment and difficult time-management situations about students sharing computers.

In some situations students are well prepared to work with computers throughout the day: They have been assigned to turn the equipment off and on and even monitor their own time on the computers. If the policy is clear and students are able to handle this efficiently and automatically, then let them proceed.

TIP

You can maintain order to the last minute of the day by calling students to line up to go home. According to your schedule, you may call walkers in only one group, bus students together, and so on. This procedure helps you avoid a mad dash as students exit for the day.

DISCIPLINE DOs

Maintain control by directing management questions to the right student and asking discreetly. To avoid asking students questions that may signal your lack of familiarity with procedures and rules ("What time is lunch?" and "Where is the stapler?"), call a calm, cooperative student to your desk and quietly ask the question to him or her individually. ("Thanks for coming so quickly, Ruth. Can you tell me where Mrs. ____ keeps her stapler?")

When you are giving instructions, stand firmly in front of the class and speak slowly and clearly. Pass out the papers yourself, or choose someone from the helper chart to assist you.

TIP

Need a helper fast? Choose the student that you think might be a troublemaker. Compliment him on his behavior (he hasn't had time to act up yet!) and ask him to help you distribute papers or supplies or carry something. (Do not send the perceived troublemaker on an errand outside of the classroom.)

Be consistent with everything you say and do. Students will trust and respond positively to teachers who follow through on what they promise (in regard to behavior, privileges, work, breaks, and so on), so you want to only make promises you can keep and then keep all of them!

Wait for silence before you begin talking. This is the number one management blunder for any teacher to avoid: Repeating yourself or yelling to make yourself heard. Say, "Boys and girls, I need your attention, please." Then wait a couple of seconds for them to look at you and get quiet. If this does not happen, stand near students who are still not listening and repeat your request. Use a calm, firm voice. If you are still having difficulty, go to the noisiest group or individual and quietly ask him to please cooperate so that you will not have to fill out any discipline forms today or send anyone to the office. Then repeat your request one more time using a calm, but firm, voice.

While you are getting the attention of the class, do not talk or give directions. Say, "I would like to see your eyes looking at me." When they are looking at you, paying attention and quiet, thank them and give your instructions clearly.

DISCIPLINE DOs continued

TIP

If you are having trouble controlling student talking, reassure students that they will have time to talk at another point in the day. You might hold up a paper that is fun or promise a group activity. Say, "I know you want to talk to each other. I will let you work in groups for the next paper (or assignment or activity). Right now, I need you to listen to me." (Or "Right now I need you to work independently without talking to anyone.") If you do say this, make sure you get around to letting them do the activity in which they can talk to others.

Model how to do the work first. Students may need help getting started with their work. Write the first problem, question, or step on the chalkboard and explain it *before* you distribute papers. Even if students know what to do, go over the first two or three steps or problems and call on students to explain what they did, what the answer was, or how they solved the problem. As they begin working, students who understand the task will *usually* be quiet, at least for a moment or two. At that time, say "Thank you for working quietly. This will make a good report to Mrs. _____ [name of teacher or principal]."

Ask for help from your buddy teacher. Most teachers will leave the name of a trusted buddy teacher on whom you can call to help you if things get tough. Do not hesitate to seek help if you are having difficulty. He or she can speak to an unruly student for you, help you complete a discipline referral, or take the unruly student into his or her classroom for a while. Getting assistance is far better than losing control of the class or getting into a power struggle with one or two students. The rest of the students usually breathe a sigh of relief once the disruptive student has been dealt with.

Watch for and acknowledge outstanding behavior. A classic example of mismanagement is that of the teacher who fills the chalkboard with names of students who have misbehaved in class. Turn this negative reinforcement technique around and watch the results. If a student is helpful (running an errand, sitting quietly, listening attentively, being helpful to another student), write his or her name on the chalkboard. Students will immediately ask you why the name is there. Say, "That is to remind me to use this name when I write my great behavior report to your teacher." You may want to be specific in your praise. "She will want to know that Amanda was helpful." "She may want to know that Amanda was kind to Carl." This works *really* well with that challenging student mentioned earlier. Continue to add names all day long. See if you can get every name up there. When the students have left for the day, write the teacher a note on the chalkboard: "Look who was great in class today!" Students will be pleased to see this compliment when they come into class the next morning.

Maintain order and quiet in the hallways. As you line your students up to leave the classroom and enter the hallway, remind them to be quiet and show good hallway manners. While you are walking along, place yourself in about the middle of the line of students so you can see both the front and the back of the line. Usually if you position yourself close to a student who is acting up, he or she will settle down.

If you see someone misbehaving, bring that student to the *front* of the line—avoid sending this student to the back, where he or she is out of your sight and is likely to get into even more trouble. You can also choose to whisper to the student, which helps him or her "save face" in front of the class. Try, "I need you to walk quietly in the hallway right now."

Now that you have read the "DOs" list, take a few minutes to read over the "DON'Ts" list. These suggestions may save you from getting into a difficult social, or even legal, situation in the future.

DISCIPLINE DON'Ts

Avoid trying to "reform" a problem student. You may run across a student whom you think you can help by using strategies to alter their behavior. However, this is not your responsibility nor is it possible to accomplish much in the short time you are with the student. Instead, focus your full attention on the entire class and how students can all work together to accomplish the day's goals.

Never try to diagnose learning or emotional problems. Other teachers and staff see this student every day. While you should report any behaviors you feel the teacher should know about, let the school staff take the lead in these situations.

Never sign legal papers unless you are directed to do so by the principal. All legal documents should be signed by the regular classroom teacher, but if you are a long-term substitute, you may be asked to attend a formal meeting to place a student into or out of a special class. If you are involved in this kind of situation and are required to give your signature, be sure to write "substitute teacher" by your name.

Avoid arguing with the rest of the staff. You may disagree with a policy or the philosophy of the school, but keep your opinions to yourself. It is the staff's responsibility to solve their own issues.

Never smoke on school property. If you smoke, find out the rules in your area before you light up. In many states you may not smoke on school property, which might include the parking lot.

DISCIPLINE DON'Ts continued

Avoid taking students anywhere that is not suggested by the regular teacher. Of course this means not leaving the campus, but it also means not eating outside at lunch time or going to the playground when it is not scheduled.

Do not bring a video from home or the rental store to show to the class. In many situations, this is illegal and the content may not be appropriate or grounded in solid academics. Show a video *only* if you are directed to do so by the classroom teacher.

Never administer any kind of medicine. Wash off minor cuts and apply bandages only. Give no medicine of any kind, even topical creams such as sunscreen. Should a student have an allergic reaction, you could be held responsible. Send students with serious cuts, bruises, or bumps to the clinic or school office.

TIP

In the smallest schools where a nurse is not available, the teacher or office staff is allowed to administer daily medications. It is rare that this would be expected of a substitute, but if you are required to do this, be sure to note the time and the dosage. Most large schools will require that students take their medications under the supervision of a qualified nurse.

Avoid giving hard candy. Many schools prohibit giving candy or cookies as a reward for work or behavior, but if the teacher has promised a treat or if you choose to purchase one, be sure to buy individually wrapped, soft, chewable, candy. You do not want to have to administer the Heimlich maneuver if hard candy becomes lodged in a student's throat. Leave gum at home. It is against the rules for students and teachers in most schools.

Avoid making physical contact with students. The most contact permissible is a quick pat on the back. Consider a big smile and a "thumbs up" as encouragement. A kind word or an offer to be the teacher's helper can give comfort and reassurance.

Avoid being alone in a room with a student. Keep your classroom door open at all times if you can, and stay with the entire group of students whenever possible.

Never leave students unsupervised. If you have a problem, call the office for help or find another adult in the building to assist you, but *always* stay with the class to which you are assigned.

End-of-the-Day Checklist

You survived! Now that your day is complete and the students are gone, take a deep breath. Follow this checklist for getting ready to leave for the day:

❑ Clean up the teacher's desk.

❑ Straighten the rows or groups of desks.

❑ Make sure the room is ready for the custodian to clean the floors.

❑ Erase or clean the chalkboard, and generally straighten the classroom (even if it wasn't straight when you walked in!).

❑ Use your own judgment about grading papers. Teachers usually appreciate the effort if you can get it done, especially if you are grading spelling papers, multiple choice, or short-response questions. You should not attempt to score essays, book reports, or long-response written answers. Avoid writing any comments on student papers. It is best to mark the number wrong (e.g., –6) at the top of the page. The teacher can do the scoring and recording while she looks to see what you accomplished.

❑ Leave the teacher a note (see sample below) or fill out a copy of the Substitute Teacher Feedback Form on page 15. She will need to know what difficulties you had, any important announcements she missed, where to find student forms or money, and what you were able to cover.

❑ If you are going to substitute in the same room tomorrow, look over the work that has been left, make any additional copies from this book, and choose a story or poem to read to the class.

❑ If a teacher or principal writes a complimentary note about your performance as a substitute, be sure to save a copy for your files. If you move to a new district, decide to go into teaching full time, or apply for a different kind of job with children, you can include it in your application.

Sample note to the teacher:

Today's date

Dear Ms. _____ ,

Thank you for having me as a substitute in your classroom today. The students were [choose one or two: helpful, cooperative, hardworking, enthusiastic]. Here is a list of the materials we covered [or did not cover]. [Write whichever list is the shortest.]

I hope you will consider recommending me to serve again as a substitute in your building.

Sincerely,
Your name

Long-Term Substituting

———————————————— • ————————————————

Most substitute jobs are for only one or two days, but there are many occasions in which substitutes are called upon to teach for a longer period of time. Here are a few suggestions for starting that kind of job.

Before Your Assignment

❑ **If you have the opportunity, spend a day with the classroom teacher.** Here you can observe how the teacher handles routine tasks like attendance, transitions to new activities, and discipline. You should begin your assignment doing things as similar to the regular routine as possible. As you become more comfortable in the classroom, you can make small adjustments, such as what time of day you check assignment books.

❑ **Meet with the classroom teacher and come up with an instructional plan for his or her absence.** For example, if the teacher was going to come back to school after the winter break, you might plan to cover mysteries and biographies in reading, up to chapter 12 in math, complete chapter 8 in social studies, and teach the solar system and electricity in science.

During Your First Weeks

❑ **Write a letter to parents to introduce yourself.** Be sure to include your school phone number or voice mail number and e-mail address. If possible, set aside one afternoon to meet parents.

❑ **If possible, meet with the other teachers on your grade level.** They will give you guidance about pacing yourself. Don't be shy about asking them for copies of engaging activities they are doing in their classrooms or for suggestions of how to handle your scheduling or discipline. Most teachers are very willing to help you out.

❑ **Make an effort to get along with the staff and participate in the school community.** Meet with the principal and offer to serve on a committee; get to know the librarian; take your turn at bus or lunch duty; hold parent conferences; and attend all staff meetings and social functions. When there is another opening at that school, they will be likely to remember your contributions to their staff.

❑ **Keep up with the paperwork.** Finding work unchecked or not graded is a big complaint among teachers returning from an absence. You don't want to leave important work for the last minute, and it is not fair for you to dump it on the returning classroom teacher.

❑ **Save copies of student work.** You can present these in portfolio style at a parent conference and you will have lots to talk about. These papers can also justify any grades you may be putting on report cards and they will be very helpful to the returning teacher.

    For particularly poor work, make a copy of the paper before sending it home. Write "Please sign and return" on the top of the page, so you will know the parent saw it. Make an indication in the grade book when these signed papers are returned to you.

❑ **Communicate with parents.** Respond to all non-urgent phone, e-mail, and written messages within 24 hours. Urgent messages about pickup arrangements or conference requests need responses as soon as possible. Schedule parent conferences as needed. You may want to have another teacher, the principal, or a guidance counselor present for the more difficult conferences.

TIP

In some situations, specific adults are the only ones allowed to pick up a student at school. The office will have that legal information on file. Do not hesitate to call them if you have any questions concerning a child's safety.

Preparing to Leave

❑ **Get things back on track.** Near the end of your assignment, begin preparing students for the return of their regular teacher. If you have changed some things in the room, change them back; if you have altered the routine, change it back. This will make the transition smoother for both the returning teacher and students.

❑ **Keep a file folder for each grade level you teach.** Include samples of activities that were particularly successful with this grade level and copies of ideas and activities that other teachers have shared with you. Write yourself notes about what you will do differently the next time you are called upon to be a long-term substitute.

❑ **Remember to thank the principal for hiring you.** He or she may have chosen from among many substitute teachers who requested long-term positions. Your thank-you note may be the key to being asked to return or being recommended for another such job.

❑ **Be aware that students often get attached to their teachers.** That may be the teacher you are replacing or it may be *you*. In either case, the transition from one teacher to another can be very difficult for certain students. Be sensitive to their needs when you first take over and when you are about to leave. Write a note to parents thanking them for their support and complimenting their children. Write a welcome back letter to the returning teacher.

Ideas for Helping Students Communicate With Their Teacher

If the teacher is out for an extended time, consider these suggestions for communicating or welcoming him or her back.

IDEA #1

Cover the chalkboard with a large sheet of bulletin board paper. Let students help you plan a scene that is seasonal, something from a field trip, or a view of the classroom. You (or the art teacher) should make general sketches of the scene in pencil while you plan where things should go. Then allow each student to draw themselves in the scene and illustrate the details. Help them write a "Get well soon," "Congratulations," or "We miss you" message. Leave it up for the teacher's return or send it to him or her in the mail.

TIP

You can make students' messages to their absent teacher extra special by adding anything to make the presentation three-dimensional, such as ribbons, raffia string, or glitter. Make the banner a keepsake by having students sign their names and write a short message.

IDEA #2

Distribute sheets of blank white paper and let each student create a page that will eventually be stapled into a book that you can give the teacher. If the teacher is out on maternity leave, let each student write a page of child-rearing advice for the new parents. ("The most important thing about raising kids is . . .") Complete by adding baby-themed decorations such as rattles around the edges of the page.

If the teacher has been ill, let each student write some "get well advice" or an "I miss you because" message. ("To get better fast, I think you should. . ." or "I wish you were back at school because . . .") Allow students to decorate the edges, then staple these into a book with a construction paper cover, and you have a nice keepsake for the returning teacher.

IDEA #3

You may want to consider weekly communication with the absent teacher. You can do this with letters, phone calls, or e-mail. This is particularly valuable if students really love and miss their regular teacher. It helps keep them connected to the teacher they love and can reassure the teacher that all is well in his or her absence.

You'll become a stronger substitute teacher as you gain experience, reflect on your successes and areas of difficulty, and apply the suggestions you have read about. As you learn, take note of the successes you've had each day, and remember that you cannot be expected to do all of these things at once and to be instantly good at all of them—great teaching takes time and lots of practice. If you get discouraged, reread the information in this section and ask yourself what were your strong and weak points—and start over in a new classroom tomorrow. (Those kids have no idea how much experience you have or what you know or do not know!)

Ready-to-Go Activities, Games, Puzzles, and More!

●

The following activities are designed for use in any situation—some require copying and others do not. They are organized by subjects and skills to help you choose an appropriate activity and report to the teacher exactly what the students worked on. Many of the reproducibles may be read aloud or used as an overhead transparency with the whole class participating, or completed by students in small groups, in pairs, or individually. You might try introducing a fact or verse from an activity in the morning and repeating the same information at the end of the day or on a successive day when you return to a classroom. See how much information the students can recall.

Language Arts/Social Studies Activities and Reproducibles

Vocabulary & Word Play

Rhymes & Riddles

Spelling

Independent and Read-Aloud Passages

Math/Science Activities and Reproducibles

Easy-to-Play Games and Quiet Activities

Language Arts/Social Studies Activities & Reproducibles

Vocabulary & Word Play

• MATCH IT! (PAGES 58–62)
Any of the pages in this section can be copied and distributed to small groups or individual students. To make any of these activities a game, consider dividing the room into halves, thirds, or fourths. As you say one piece of information (the first name of a president or the name of an adult animal), have the groups guess the corresponding answer correctly (the president's last name or the name of the baby animal). Allow the groups to talk it over and ask one member to respond with the answer. On the chalkboard score one point for each correct answer. The game can be continued later in the day or even on the following day. (Note: By conducting the game in this way, you have taken pressure off of any one student who might not be able to respond alone.) Remind groups to hold their discussions to a whisper so that others will not hear their answers. You can further control the noise level by telling the class that you will ask a question, but if the group having the turn misses it, the next group will get a chance to try for the answer.

If students need reference material for the more difficult questions (such as the names of presidents), allow the team members to use their science or social studies textbooks. Be sure to direct them to the reference pages in those sources so they will know where to look for charts, lists, and maps.

• IDIOMS ADD SPICE TO OUR LANGUAGE AND IDIOM CROSSWORD FUN (PAGES 63–66)
An idiom is a saying that means something very different from its literal meaning. Introduce idioms with this example: When we say, "It's raining cats and dogs," we really mean that it is raining very hard. There are not cats or dogs falling from the sky! (*Note:* There are hundreds of idioms in our language. To learn the history and origin of each one, check out *Scholastic Dictionary of Idioms* by Marvin Terban (Scholastic, 1996).

Challenge students to write or illustrate other idioms they know. To make the crossword puzzles more difficult, fold back or cover the suggested list at the bottom of the page before making copies.

Rhymes & Riddles

• CRACK THE CODE! (PAGE 67)
The following poem appeared in the July 1903 issue of *Woman's Home Companion.* Make copies of this page to distribute to students or better yet, copy it onto a sheet of chart paper and take it with you from school to school. Students will have great fun trying to figure out what it says. Let them in on the trick—read it out loud and just say the letters as you come to them. Help students practice cursive handwriting by copying the poem and spelling out the decoded words.

• MOTHER GOOSE RHYME TIME (PAGE 68)
Students will enjoy hearing a longer version of this classic poem (Note: Two stanzas have been cut). Help them see that there are two ways to guess the missing word. Synonyms below the fill-in lines offer a hint and the missing word must rhyme in the stanza. When they've discovered the missing words, have the class read it aloud. Make sure students understand the last verse, which is intended to be a joke. We usually think of dogs serving humans, but in this case, the woman plays the servant to the dog.

• LIMERICK FUN (PAGE 69)
Have students learn the cadence and pattern of limericks. How many lines are there? (5) Which words rhyme in every pattern? (Words at the end of lines 1, 2, and 5 rhyme; words at the end of lines 3 and 4 rhyme.) Do they notice that the last word in the first line is the same as the last word in the fifth line? How many syllables are in each line? (It varies! Line 1 always has eight syllables; line 2 has eight or nine; line 3 has six or seven;

line 4 has five or six; and line 5 has eight or nine.) You can teach students to count syllables by having them drum their fingers or clap softly while they count—one clap or touch for each syllable that they say.

Challenge students to follow the established patterns of rhyming words and syllables and be creative as they finish the limerick starters provided.

Allow students to work in teams or small groups (3 or 4). Time left over? Let them illustrate their limericks.

Hint: If you get the sense from the class that students might create a limerick that uses inappropriate language or references, announce ahead of time that you may post these on a bulletin board or share them with the principal or the returning teacher.

Spelling

• THE CASE OF THE FROG PRINCE AND THE CASE OF THE TERRIBLE TOOTH FAIRY (PAGES 70–71)

You might read aloud these funny adventures of two storybook characters, adapted from *Storyworks Magazine*'s "Grammar Cop," before handing out copies. Have students find all the mistakes on each page and complete the list. Let younger students or students who need more support work in groups.

Reading Passages for Independent Reading or Read-Aloud

• "THE ANIMAL THIEVES" (PAGES 72–73)

Persuasive writing is intended to urge someone to act in a certain way or to convince them to agree with a point of view. "The Animal Thieves" is an example of this kind of nonfiction writing. This article asks students to look at why animal smuggling is wrong. Copy and distribute the article to students. Let them read it independently or in pairs. Either discuss the follow-up questions with students as a group or have them write their responses independently.

You might also assign the written part as homework.

• "THE WONDERFUL PIED PIPER" (PAGES 74–75)

Share this classic tale with your students when you have about 15 minutes to fill. After reading it aloud, lead a lively discussion about the story or allow students to illustrate what they heard. Then ask the following discussion questions: What life lessons does this story present? (To be a person of your word; to pay your debts; not to make promises that you do not intend to keep.) What expressions have you heard in our modern language that relate to this tale? (Time to pay the piper; The pied piper of Hamelin.)

• "THE BLUE CARBUNCLE" (PAGES 76–79)

Use this play to introduce students to the famous detective Mr. Sherlock Holmes, and his assistant, Dr. Watson. In the opening scene, Mr. Holmes is making some deductions about a character just by looking at his hat. It is this power of deduction that made Holmes so famous. Make sure students understand that Holmes makes his assumptions about Mr. Baker from only the small clues found on the hat. As the story ends, Holmes uses this power of deduction to find the thief in the story. See if students can tell how he knew it was Mr. James Ryder that stole the gem. (He worked at the hotel, knew Catherine Cusak, and was nervous and anxious to find out about the goose.)

Hints for a class read-aloud: You can make reading this play extra fun for students by assigning parts. If you have a large group of students, switch part assignments for each scene. Be sure to allow students to read through the story at least one time (possibly with a reading buddy) so they will not be embarrassed when called upon to read aloud.

You may or may not need to "grade" student's work. Allow students to complete the activity page with a partner or two, or complete it as a whole group project and solicit group discussion about the questions.

Math/Science Activities & Reproducibles

• INTERSECTING SHAPES & NUMBERS (PAGE 80) Students can trace the three shapes in any three different colors. This will help them organize the numbers spatially and reinforce basic geometry. You might also draw the intersecting shapes larger on the board for students who may need extra support. Review the two operations terms that students will encounter: *sum* (which signals addition) and *difference* (which signals subtraction).

• GOING ON A FIELD TRIP #1 AND #2 (PAGES 81–84) Here are two sets of story problems about students on a fictional field trip. These are very much alike, but the first one is easier than the second. Make sure students show their work. Encourage them to circle key words that helped them decide which operation to use, including *sum, in all* (addition), *difference, more than, larger than, longer than* (subtraction), *each* (multiplication/division).

• TANGRAM PUZZLER (PAGE 85) This ancient puzzle provides spatial and logical challenges for kids of all ages. If possible, run copies of the puzzle on construction paper, oak tag paper, or card stock. Ask them what shapes they see in the large square. Their response should be: a large square containing one smaller square, two large triangles, one medium triangle, two small triangles, and one parallelogram (more specifically, a rhombus). Have students point to each one as it is discussed so that you are sure they have found all of the parts. You may want to discuss the characteristics of each shape as you do so. (How do you know it is a triangle? What are the characteristics of a square?) Then instruct students to cut out the shapes carefully along the solid lines. When they have finished, challenge them to make these pieces back into a square. Then let them try to re-create the shapes on the sides using all of the tangram pieces. (Answers on page 96.) If you are going to be in the same room again, have each student store his or her pieces in a plastic sandwich bag. Next time challenge them to make their own tangram creations, trace the outline of the shape, and hand it to a classmate to solve.

• 100S CHART PATTERNS (PAGES 86–87) Hundreds charts activities like the ones here help students find patterns in numbers. They also take a long time to complete and can give you a needed rest or buy you some time to plan your next activity. Let students choose four patterns to color in from the activity list on page 86. Distribute extra copies of the charts on page 87 for students who finish early and have them create their own number pattern or choose another pattern from the activity list. You might point out that when the students are "counting by threes" they are really just "doing" their threes multiplication table!

Hint: Need more 100's charts? Students can easily make their own in a 10-by-10 unit square on graph paper, numbering 1–100 in rows from top left to bottom right.

• WHALES AND DOLPHINS (PAGES 88–89) Students at this age love animals—especially the giants of the sea. After reading this article, help students complete the accompanying activity sheet to practice several skills that are regularly tested on state and national assessments. These skills include recall of facts, identifying fact and opinion, and recognizing comparisons made by the author.

• GET THE PICTURE? (PAGE 90) Students get absorbed deeply in this visual discrimination and decoding activity. Even older students will enjoy discovering how the colored grid square "pixels" merge together at a distance to reveal sharks! The best thing about this activity is that students can actually see how a computer screen works.

Match It! States & Capitals

Name _____   Date _____

Directions: Match the name of the capital city to its state.

1. California	_____	**2.** Ohio	_____
3. West Virginia	_____	**4.** Vermont	_____
5. Kansas	_____	**6.** Arizona	_____
7. Texas	_____	**8.** New York	_____
9. Nevada	_____	**10.** New Mexico	_____
11. Tennessee	_____	**12.** Louisiana	_____
13. New Jersey	_____	**14.** Alaska	_____
15. Connecticut	_____	**16.** Hawaii	_____
17. Kentucky	_____	**18.** Massachusetts	_____
19. Montana	_____	**20.** Nebraska	_____
21. Oregon	_____	**22.** South Carolina	_____
23. Pennsylvania	_____	**24.** New Hampshire	_____
25. Wisconsin	_____	**26.** Washington	_____
27. Utah	_____	**28.** Georgia	_____
29. Mississippi	_____	**30.** Michigan	_____
31. Maryland	_____	**32.** Maine	_____
33. Iowa	_____	**34.** Illinois	_____
35. Indiana	_____	**36.** Florida	_____
37. Delaware	_____	**38.** Colorado	_____
39. Arkansas	_____	**40.** Alabama	_____
41. Wyoming	_____	**42.** Virginia	_____
43. South Dakota	_____	**44.** Minnesota	_____
45. North Carolina	_____	**46.** North Dakota	_____
47. Idaho	_____	**48.** Oklahoma	_____
49. Rhode Island	_____	**50.** Missouri	_____

The Substitute Teacher Resource Book • Scholastic Teaching Resources

Name _____   **Date** _____

A. Nashville   **B.** Charleston

C. Santa Fe   **D.** Springfield

E. Annapolis   **F.** Montgomery

G. Juneau   **H.** Phoenix

I. Little Rock   **J.** Sacramento

K. Denver   **L.** Augusta

M. Oklahoma City   **N.** Montpelier

O. Pierre   **P.** Richmond

Q. Cheyenne   **R.** Olympia

S. Helena   **T.** St. Paul

U. Atlanta   **V.** Lansing

W. Jefferson City   **X.** Albany

Y. Jackson   **Z.** Raleigh

AA. Madison   **BB.** Austin

CC. Baton Rouge   **DD.** Hartford

EE. Columbus   **FF.** Tallahassee

GG. Des Moines   **HH.** Frankfort

II. Boston   **JJ.** Providence

KK. Salem   **LL.** Columbia

MM. Harrisburg   **NN.** Topeka

OO. Indianapolis   **PP.** Honolulu

QQ. Boise   **RR.** Bismarck

SS. Salt Lake City   **TT.** Dover

UU. Trenton   **VV.** Lincoln

WW. Carson City   **XX.** Concord

The Substitute Teacher Resource Book • Scholastic Teaching Resources

Match It! Who Wrote Which Book?

Name _____   **Date** _____

Hint: You'll find two book titles for two of the authors listed.

Directions: Match the title of each best-selling children's book to its author.

1. *The Tale of Peter Rabbit*

J. K. Rowling ➡

2. *The Cat in the Hat*

H. A. Rey ➡

3. *Where the Sidewalk Ends*

E. B. White ➡

4. *Winnie the Pooh*

Dr. Seuss ➡

5. *Harry Potter and the Sorcerer's Stone*

Gertrude Chandler Warner ➡

6. *Charlotte's Web*

Eric Carle ➡

7. *Tales of a Fourth Grade Nothing*

Laura Ingalls Wilder ➡

8. *Little House on the Prairie*

Tomie de Paola ➡

9. *Freckle Juice*

Ezra Jack Keats ➡

10. *Brown Bear, Brown Bear, What Do You See?*

Shel Silverstein ➡

11. *Caps for Sale*

James Marshall ➡

12. *Where the Wild Things Are*

Leo Lionni ➡

13. *Miss Nelson Is Missing*

Maurice Sendak ➡

14. *The Snowy Day*

Beatrix Potter ➡

15. *Swimmy*

Esphyr Slobodkina ➡

16. *500 Hats of Bartholomew Cubbins*

A. A. Milne ➡

17. *The Boxcar Children*

Judy Blume ➡

18. *Strega Nona*

Patricia MacLachlan ➡

19. *Curious George*

20. *Sarah Plain and Tall*

Name _____   Date _____

If you have a familiar name like Emily or Michael, you may think some of our presidents have had very unusual names.

Directions: Match the first (or middle) and last names of these Presidents of the United States.

Hint: Look it up! The names of presidents can be found in almanacs, your social studies book, an encyclopedia, and even in some dictionaries.

First or Middle Name	**Last Name**
Brichard ✴	Kennedy
Herbert ✴	Roosevelt
Ulysses ✴	Adams
Delano ✴	Fillmore
Calvin ✴	Hayes
Quincy ✴	Cleveland
Knox ✴	Polk
Millard ✴	Johnson
Fitzgerald ✴	Grant
Milhouse ✴	Coolidge
Abram ✴	Hoover
Grover ✴	Ford
Rudolph ✴	Garfield
Earl ✴	Nixon
Baines ✴	Carter

The Substitute Teacher Resource Book • Scholastic Teaching Resources

What Is the **N**ame of the Group?

Name _____ **Date** _____

You may know that a bunch of fish is called a "school," but can you match other animals with their group names?

Directions: Use the word choices in the box to fill in the blanks.

Example: **1.** a flock of ___pigeons___

2. a bed of _____

3. a colony of _____

4. a leap of _____

5. a plague of _____

6. a pride of _____

7. a school of _____

8. a swarm of _____

9. a troop of _____

10. a murder of _____

11. a pod of _____

12. a clowder of _____

13. a covey of _____

14. a knot of _____

15. a rafter of _____

16. a gaggle of _____

17. a crash of _____

18. a parliament of _____

Animal Choices

monkeys, cats, ants, pigeons, geese, leopards, fish, owls, kittens,
turkeys, frogs, locusts, quail, clams or oysters, lions, bees,
rhinoceroses, crows, seals, whales

The Substitute Teacher Resource Book • Scholastic Teaching Resources

Idioms—The **S**pice in Our Language

Name _____ **Date** _____

An idiom is a phrase or saying that has taken on a meaning different from what the words actually say. For example, "My goldfish kicked the bucket" does not mean that the fish jumped out of the fish tank, ran across the room, and knocked his flipper against a bucket. It means that the fish died.

Directions: Write a short phrase or sentence explaining what the following idioms mean in your own words. Then choose three to illustrate in cartoons on the back of this page.

1. *"He has ants in his pants,"* laughed the father of the wriggling three-year-old.

_____

2. Don't just sit there *like a bump on a log.* _____

3. "Don't *spill the beans*," warned my aunt who was planning a surprise party for

my sister. _____

4. Four-leaf clovers are *as scarce as hen's teeth.* _____

5. Maybe after that accident, he'll *turn over a new leaf.* _____

_____

6. The boy who won tickets to the car show was walking *on cloud nine.* _____

_____

7. We got soaked on our walk to school. It was *raining cats and dogs.*

_____

8. That buzzing noise will *drive me up the wall.* _____

9. We knew she was feeling fine—she was crying *crocodile tears.*

_____

10. The problem is over now. There's no use *crying over spilled milk.*

_____

11. I didn't do it! You are *barking up the wrong tree.* _____

12. When the guilty child didn't answer, his older sister asked, "Has the *cat got your*

tongue?" _____

13. I've had it! I'm *at the end of my rope.* _____

14. His aim is so bad, he *can't hit the side of a barn.* _____

_____

15. Those shoes *cost an arm and a leg.* _____

The Substitute Teacher Resource Book • Scholastic Teaching Resources

Name _____ Date _____

You probably don't think much about it, but you are constantly talking about your clothes. Not the clothes you have on, but clothes in general.

Directions: Fill in the blank in the following expressions using the correct article of clothing and then complete the puzzle.

ACROSS

1. My dad is the boss at our house. He wears the _____ in the family.

2. Mom was busy in the craft room. Dad said she had a bee in her _____ .

3. Coach Thompson was hot under the _____ when we lost the football game.

4. All of the girls in Tracy's class got together and had a _____ party.

6. Grandpa doesn't give any hints about the cards in his hand. He plays it close to the _____ .

7. Reuben won the piano competition this year. The award was a feather in his _____ .

9. Greta's family did not have much money. For a while they were living on a _____ .

11. Zach just won't grow up. He is still tied to his mother's _____ strings.

DOWN

1. Someone who steals your wallet without you even knowing is called a pick-_____.

2. My little brother thinks he is really grown up, but my mom says he is too big for his _____ .

5. Be careful! Don't get stung by that yellow _____ .

8. Malcolm left our team to play for the Panthers. He is a turn-_____ .

10. That coat is perfect for you. It fits like a _____ .

Answer Box

pocket, coat, jacket, pajama, cap, glove, collar, bonnet, pants, shoestring, britches, apron, vest

---

The Substitute Teacher Resource Book • Scholastic Teaching Resources

Idiom Crossword Fun: Animals

Name _____ **Date** _____

Our language is filled with funny expressions that include animal names.

Directions: Fill in the blanks in the following expressions using the correct animal name and then complete the puzzle. One answer is used two times.

ACROSS

1. The game you play where you jump over someone's back is called leap-_____ .

3. I know something is wrong here. I smell a _____ .

5. I knew Jimmy could _____ his way out of doing any work.

8. If you eat really fast, your dad might tell you not to _____ down your food.

10. We won by a score of 12–0. We really _____ed them!

12. When you lose your nerve, we say you _____ out.

14. We had to _____ through the crowd to get to the stage.

DOWN

2. You are a tattletale if you _____ on your friend.

4. My older brother warned, "When he asks you what happened, don't tell. Just _____ up."

6. Joey never spends his own money. He likes to _____ off of other people.

7. Do not let the toddler _____ with the computer.

9. I know Sandra. She will _____ me until I give in.

11. If the ball comes toward you, be sure to _____ your head.

13. People who eat a lot and sloppily eat like a _____ .

Answer Box

wolf, chicken, horse, snake, duck, hound, clam,
weasel, skunk, monkey, rat, frog, sponge

The Substitute Teacher Resource Book • Scholastic Teaching Resources

Idiom Crossword Fun: Food

Name _____ Date _____

We really like to eat! We like food so much that we mention things we eat all the time—even when we're not talking about food or eating!

Directions: Fill in the blank in the following expressions with the correct food word and then complete the puzzle. One answer is used two times.

ACROSS

2. I beat my little sister at Monopoly. It was like taking _____ from a baby.

4. My mom works and gets paid for it. We say she "brings home the _____ ."

8. Peggy doesn't know _____ about multiplication.

10. Long division is a tough _____ to crack.

11. That game is so easy, it's a piece of _____ .

12. If you watch too much television, you might be called a couch _____ .

13. If your teacher really likes you, we say you are the _____ of her eye.

14. Jack finally finished his homework, but he was as slow as _____ .

DOWN

1. I heard the kids went crazy at the party. Mr. Smith said they went _____ .

3. There were no sneakers left. The salesclerk said they were selling like _____ .

5. The crazy lady next door was as nutty as a _____ .

6. If your lunch bag is on the bottom of the pile, your sandwich may be as flat as a _____ .

7. If you don't know what to do next, we say you are in a _____ .

8. To keep you from telling a secret, we warn you not to spill the _____ .

9. The bus was really crowded. We were packed in there like _____ .

Answer Box
sardines, fruitcake, pickle, bacon, beans, candy, bananas, hotcakes, apple, nut, potato, pancake, cake, molasses

The Substitute Teacher Resource Book • Scholastic Teaching Resources

Crack the Code!

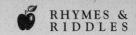

Name _____   **Date** _____

Directions: Some of the words in this poem have been replaced with pairs of letters that sound like the missing words. Can you figure out what word belongs in place of each underlined letter pair? Try reading the poem out loud and saying the names of the letters as you come to them.

Hint: Some letter pairs stand for two words.

The farmer leads no **EZ** life.   _____

The **CD** sows will rot;   _____

And when at **EV** rests from strife,   _____

His bones will **AK** lot.   _____

In **DD** has to struggle hard   _____

To **EK** living out;   _____

If **IC** frosts do not retard   _____

His crops, there'll **BA** drought.   _____

The hired **LP** has to pay   _____

Are awful **AZ**, too;   _____

They **CK** rest when he's away,   _____

Nor **NE** work will do.   _____

*What do you think the farmer did when his helpers did not work and his farm was failing? Write one or two stanzas to tell how the story should end. Try to follow the **4MAT** of the poem.*

_____

_____

_____

_____

_____

_____

_____

The Substitute Teacher Resource Book • Scholastic Teaching Resources

Mother Goose Rhyme Time

Name _____   **Date** _____

Directions: Write in the missing words to this old favorite rhyme. The synonyms below each line offer clues. The word you choose must also fit the rhyming pattern of the poem.

Old Mother Hubbard

Old Mother Hubbard
Went to the cupboard
To get her poor _____ a bone;
       pet (canine)
But when she came there
The cupboard was _____ ,
       empty
And so the poor _____ had none.
       pet (canine)

She went to the fishmonger's
To buy him some fish,
And when she came back
He was licking the _____ .
       plate

She went to the hatter's
To buy him a hat,
But when she came back
He was feeding her _____ .
       pet (feline)

She went to the barber's
To buy him a wig,
But when she came back
He was dancing a _____ .
       lively dance

She went to the fruiterer's
To buy him some fruit,
But when she came back
He was playing the _____ .
       woodwind instrument

She went to the tailor's
To buy him a _____ ,
       jacket
But when she came back
He was riding a goat.

She went to the cobbler's
To buy him some _____ ,
       footwear
But when she came back
He was reading the news.

She went to the hosier's
To buy him some hose
But when she came back
He was dressed in his _____ .
       garments

The dame made a curtsy,
The dog made a bow;
The dame said, "Your servant,"
The dog said," Bow, _____ ."
       exclamation

The Substitute Teacher Resource Book • Scholastic Teaching Resources

Limerick **Fun**

Name _____   **Date** _____

Directions: Read the limericks below. Notice that each has a pattern of five lines with a set pattern of beats per line. Say them out loud and quietly clap out the syllables. Choose a limerick starter and use it as the first line of your limerick or invent your own. Write your limerick on the back of this page.

There was an Old Person of Dean
Who dined on one pea and one bean;
For he said, "More than that,
Would make me too fat,"
That cautious Old Person of Dean.

There was a Young Lady whose chin
Resembled the point of a pin;
So she had it made sharp,
And purchased a harp,
And played several tunes with her chin.

There was a Young Lady whose nose
Was so long that it reached to her toes;
So she hired an Old Lady,
Whose conduct was steady,
To carry that wonderful nose.

There was an Old Man in a boat,
Who said, "I'm afloat! I'm afloat!"
When they said, 'No, you ain't!"
He was ready to faint,
That unhappy Old Man in a boat.

There was an Old Man in a tree,
Who was horribly bored by a Bee.
When they said, "Does it buzz?"
He replied, "Yes, it does!
It's a regular brute of a Bee."

Limerick Starters:

There was a Young Boy with a bike …

There once was a Young Girl named Kate …

There was a Young Gentleman Tom …

There was an Old Woman whose hair …

Limericks by Edward Lear (From *A Book of Nonsense* by Edward Lear. Boston: Little, Brown, 1891).

The Substitute Teacher Resource Book • Scholastic Teaching Resources

The Case of the Frog Prince

 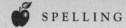

Name _____ **Date** _____

Ever since Prince Leonardo was turned into a frog, his spelling skills have really suffered. His letter below is filled with spelling errors. Can you help him?

Hint: There are 20 misspelled words.

Directions: Circle each misspelled word. Then write down the correct spelling in the spaces provided below.

Dear Madam Witch,

I am writting to you to tell you how dissapointed I am that you have refussed to tern me back into a prince. I have apoligized over and over agian for making that little coment about the wart on your nose. I have suffered enougf! If you don't think so, turn yourself into a frog and see what it is like. I must share my pond with three verry nasty geese. The pond water is recking my skin. And the food is terible (altho I did catch a most delishous fly yesterday for lunch). I miss my palase!

In your last letter, you told me that the spell will be broken when a princess gives me a kiss. I am afrade that there is a real shortage of princesses around the kingdom. Most are off at collige. If a princess did happen to see me at the pond, I somehow dout she would want to kiss me.

Please, won't you reconsidder? You know wear to find me: on the second rock to the rite.

Best wishes,

Prince Leonardo
(The geese call me Prince Slimo)

P.S. If you turn me back into a prince, I'll pay the finest doctor to take care of that little problem in your nasal area.

© Grammar Cop, Scholastic, 2004.

1. _____

2. _____

3. _____

4. _____

5. _____

6. _____

7. _____

8. _____

9. _____

10. _____

11. _____

12. _____

13. _____

14. _____

15. _____

16. _____

17. _____

18. _____

19. _____

20. _____

The Substitute Teacher Resource Book • Scholastic Teaching Resources

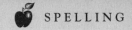 SPELLING

Name _____ **Date** _____

There are problems in Tooth Fairy Land. This letter will be sent to the queen, but it's filled with spelling mistakes! Can you help?

Directions: Circle the misspelled words in the letter below. Write them correctly in the blanks provided below.

Hint: There are 15 misspelled words.

1. _____

2. _____

3. _____

4. _____

5. _____

6. _____

7. _____

8. _____

9. _____

10. _____

11. _____

12. _____

13. _____

14. _____

15. _____

TO: Queen Tooth Fairy
FROM: Complaint Bureau

Over the past month, I have recieved five complaints about tooth fairy number 324, also known as Doris. Last Friday, on a job in Montana, she stopped in the kichen and made herself a lettuce and wipped cream sandwish. She left a big mess. Then, she took a nap in the kid's dollhouse.

Afterwords, she turned on a Backstreet Boys CD and started dansing on the bed. The little girl woke up and started screeming. The mother thought Doris was a giant mosquito and went after her with a can of bug spray. Doris escaped, but we nearley had a disaster. I don't have to tell you what would happen if the newspapers herd about this.

As you know, all tooth fairies are trained at the Tooth Fairy Command Center. The rules are clear. They are to fly into a room quietley and carfully inspect the tooth under the pillow, without waking up the child. If they beleive the tooth is real (fake teeth are a growing probblem) they are to leave 50 cents. They are then to exit the house without making any noise.

Doris is a hopeless case. I believe you should help her find a job with anuther organization. I undorstand the Easter Bunny needs some help this year.

© Grammar Cop, Scholastic, 2004.

The Substitute Teacher Resource Book • Scholastic Teaching Resources

Name _____   Date _____

Directions: Read the following article and look for how the author makes her argument.

The Animal Thieves

Selling Illegal Pets Is Big Business

His name is Anson Wong, and he was one of the world's most dangerous thieves. He didn't rob banks or steal jewels. He stole animals from the wild—endangered and deadly animals. His specialty was the Komodo dragon, the world's largest land lizard. Wong earned millions of dollars selling his stolen animals to collectors around the world.

Wildlife experts celebrated last December when Wong was finally caught and put in jail. But animal smuggling remains a huge—and growing—problem around the world. "There are people in the United States and around the world who want to own exotic animals as pets," says Craig Hoover, an expert who works for the World Wildlife Fund. "As long as there are people willing to pay thousands of dollars for these animals, there will be people like Anson Wong willing to smuggle the animals out of the wild."

Dozens of different bird and reptile species are the victims of this illegal business. Endangered breeds of parrots, rare giant lizards and tortoises, and deadly snakes are especially popular with collectors.

Smugglers steal the animals or eggs from native habitats like jungles and rain forests. They then sneak them into countries where they can be sold as pets. Their smuggling methods are often cruel.

"They pack snakes and lizards into suitcases and drug birds before stuffing them into tires or tennis ball cans," says Hoover. "These people will do anything." Of course, many animals die during their journeys.

This business has hurt many animal populations. "Thieves will go into a rain forest and steal hundreds of eggs from a single area," says Hoover. For a species already threatened or endangered, this kind of theft can be devastating.

Animal smuggling endangers humans as well. Often someone will buy an exotic animal without having any idea how to care for it. Every year, for example, dozens of people in the United States are bitten by deadly snakes that were sold illegally as pets. One Florida man died last year from a cobra bite.

"This is an evil business," says Don Bruning, a bird specialist who works at the Wildlife Conservation Society in New York City. "It's wonderful that people are interested in unusual animals. But no one should be selling endangered or dangerous animals. And no matter how much money a person has to spend, they should never be able to buy a priceless part of our natural world."

© *Storyworks*, Scholastic, 2002.

The Substitute Teacher Resource Book • Scholastic Teaching Resources

Name _____ **Date** _____

Directions: Please use complete sentences to answer the following questions.

The Animal Thieves: Follow Up

1. Before he was caught and jailed, how did Anson Wong make his living?

_____

_____

_____

_____

2. Tell how animal smuggling is cruel to the animals.

_____

_____

_____

_____

3. Tell why animal smuggling is bad for planet Earth.

_____

_____

_____

_____

4. Mr. Wong made millions of dollars. Why was Mr. Wong so successful?

_____

_____

_____

_____

5. What is the author trying to persuade *you*, the reader, to do or not to do?

_____

_____

_____

The Substitute Teacher Resource Book • Scholastic Teaching Resources

A very long time ago a strange thing happened in the little town called Hamelin. There were so many rats in the town that the people did not know what to do. The rats were everywhere. They tried to get rid of the rats using cats and dogs and traps and poisons, but none of them seemed to do any good. The rats became worse every day.

One Friday a pied* stranger came into town. He had a crooked nose, a long mustache, and two great gray eyes that twinkled and shone under the broad brim of his hat. He was dressed in a green jacket with a leather belt and short red trousers that were buckled at the knee. Stuck in the top of his hat was a long red feather and on his feet were sandals fastened by strings around his legs.

Nobody knew where this strange man came from. He was walking down the street playing Scottish bagpipes and singing this song:

"Oh, don't you see
that this is he
Who has come to free
Your town from rats?

"Ere another day
if you will but say,
I'll drive away
Your troublesome rats."

The Wise Men of the town heard his song and asked the stranger if he could help them. The stranger said that if they would pay him, he would drive every rat out of Hamelin before morning of the next day.

The Mayor spoke up. "It is plain to me that this is the wizard who sent us the rats and now he wants to drive them away for our money. We must learn to catch a wizard in his own trap. Bring this wizard to me."

When the stranger stood in front of the mayor he said, "I will agree to rid the town of rats by morning if you will pay me a groschen** for each head."

"You ask too much," said the Wise Men. "There are thousands of rats. It will take all of our silver."

But the Mayor said, "All right, my good man. We will pay you a groschen a head."

The stranger said, "I will work as soon as the sun is set. Keep all of the people of the town in their houses, but they may look out of their windows to see a pleasant sight."

When the sun set, the piper began to play another tune. It started out sweet and low at first and then became more and more lively until it was loud and shrill. From all of the houses and basements and alleys the rats began to leap. They ran into the streets and covered the roads like rushing water. They cared for nothing but the piper and his strange music and followed them as if they were blind.

Then the piper turned and walked to the river. He kept playing on his pipes and the great army of rats followed him. Then the piper cried, "Hop! Hop!" and all of the rats hopped into the river and were seen no more.

The next morning the Wise Men of Hamelin were sitting in the town hall. "The rats are gone and the town is saved, but now we must pay the piper. It is a

The Substitute Teacher Resource Book • Scholastic Teaching Resources

great price for getting rid of the rats."

Just then the piper came into the hall. "All of your rats have jumped into the river and not one of them shall ever come back. There were nine hundred ninety-nine thousand nine hundred and ninety-nine of the animals. You can easily reckon how much to pay me at one groschen a head."

"That is right," said the Mayor, "but I must see the heads to count them. Where are they?"

The piper saw that a trick was being played on him and he cried, "You know all of the rats are dead in the river. If you want their heads, go to the river and find them."

"Well, we will not pay you unless you show us their heads."

"Then," said the piper, "Since you will not pay me, I will be paid by your heirs.***" He pulled his hat down over his eyes and left the hall.

"That is the way to deal with wizards," said the Mayor. "We have caught him in his own trap."

But the Wise Men wondered what the piper meant by his strange words.

The next day was Sunday and all of the men and women of Hamelin went to church. As they left the church they all remarked about how pleasant it was to walk along the streets without tripping over the rats. Then they began to wonder where were all of the children that were usually seen in the yards and in the doorways. They began to call out for their own children, but no children could they find. The parents were frantic and ran through the streets calling, "Where are our children?"

Finally they found one little boy, Jacob. He was crippled and was hobbling along on his crutches. He began to cry as he told his story. While all of the adults were in church, the piper returned and began to play the most wonderful music. Every boy and girl ran out of their houses and up the streets to hear it. Then they went singing and dancing out the east gate of town. Jacob said he tried to go, but he couldn't keep up because of his crutches.

The people of Hamelin mounted their horses and looked everywhere for their children, but none of them were ever seen again. About their Mayor they only said, "If he had been a man honest and true, this thing would not have happened."

The people of Hamelin will tell you that this sad thing happened on a midsummer day in the year 1284. If you ever go there, you will see on a window of the great church, a picture of the piper, dressed in his colorful clothes. The street through which the piper led children is still pointed out to strangers. On that street, no one is permitted to play any sort of musical instrument, even to this very day.

* Pied means "variegated with spots of different colors," as were the piper's clothes. Hence the name, "The Pied Piper."

** A groschen is a piece of silver worth about five cents.

*** An heir is someone who will inherit money and possessions when someone dies. In this case, the heirs were the children.

Story adapted from *Baldwin's Readers* ©1897, American Book Company.

The Substitute Teacher Resource Book • Scholastic Teaching Resources

The Blue Carbuncle

Name _____ Date _____

Adapted from the short story by Arthur Conan Doyle

CHARACTERS:

SHERLOCK HOLMES—the famous detective
DOCTOR WATSON—a medical doctor that assists Holmes
PETERSON—the police commissionaire
MR. HENRY BAKER—the man who has lost his goose
MR. WINDIGATE—owner of a pub called the Alpha Club
MR. JAMES RYDER—a worker at the Hotel Cosmopolitan
MR. JOHN HORNER—a plumber at the Hotel Cosmopolitan
COUNTESS OF MORCAR—a famous Countess who has lost a precious stone
CATHERINE CUSAK—maid to the Countess
NARRATORS

SCENE ONE
In the apartment of Sherlock Holmes

NARRATOR: One December day, Dr. Watson visited his friend Sherlock Holmes. Entering his apartment he found Holmes staring at a top hat, which was hanging on the back of a straight chair.

WATSON: Are you busy, Holmes?

SHERLOCK HOLMES: Not at all. I have an interesting problem to study.

WATSON: Where did you get the hat?

HOLMES: The facts are these: About four o'clock on Christmas morning, Peterson, the police commissionaire, was returning home from a party. Walking in front of him, he saw a tall man carrying a white goose. Then he witnessed a fight between this man and a gang. When the stranger saw the commissionaire, he lost his hat, dropped the goose, and ran away. Peterson noticed a small tag on the leg of the goose. It said "For Mrs. Henry Baker." He brought the goose and the hat to me, hoping that I could help to find the rightful owner.

WATSON: So where is the goose now?

HOLMES: I gave it to Peterson so that it might fulfill the ultimate destiny of a goose.

WATSON: So, how will you find the owner of the hat? There are certainly several Henry Bakers in London.

HOLMES: By studying it, of course. Here, use my lens. *(Hands Watson a magnifying glass.)*

WATSON: But I can see nothing extraordinary about the hat.

HOLMES: On the contrary, Watson. You can see everything. You fail, however, to reason from what you see.

WATSON: Then, pray tell, what can you infer from this hat?

(Holmes picks up the hat and studies it carefully.)

HOLMES: The owner of this hat was highly intellectual and fairly well-to-do within the last three years, although he has now fallen upon hard times. His wife has ceased to love him. He is a man who does not get much exercise, and is out of shape. He does not go out much, is middle-aged, has grizzled hair, and has just had a haircut. Also, he has just begun to light his house with gas.

WATSON: My dear Mr. Holmes! I am unable to follow you.

HOLMES: You know my method, Watson. *(Holmes puts on the hat, which covers most of his face.)* A man with a head this large must have a large brain, and therefore must be very smart. This man could afford this expensive hat three years ago, but has not had a new one since, so he must have lost

The Substitute Teacher Resource Book • Scholastic Teaching Resources

his money. I can see traces of sweat, meaning that he is out of shape and perspires a lot when he walks. There are short hairs like those that are left just after a haircut. The hat is dusty, meaning that the owner does not get out much, and it has not been brushed, meaning that his wife has ceased to care about his appearance. There are no candle stains on the hat, so he must have been lighting his home with gas instead of candles.

WATSON: That is very ingenious, but since there was no crime committed and no harm done except the loss of a goose, this seems to be a waste of energy.

NARRATOR: Sherlock Holmes was about to reply to Watson's remark about the waste of his energies when suddenly the door burst open and in dashed Peterson, the commissionaire. He was quite excited and his face was dazed in astonishment.

PETERSON: The goose, Mr. Holmes! The goose, sir!

HOLMES: What of it then? Has it returned to life and flown off through the kitchen window?

PETERSON: See here, sir! See what my wife has found in its crop!

NARRATOR: Peterson held out his hand to reveal a brilliantly scintillating blue stone, smaller than a bean, but of such purity and radiance that it twinkled like an electric point in the hollow of his hand.

HOLMES: By Jove, Peterson, this is a treasure-trove indeed! I suppose you know what you have got?

PETERSON: A diamond, sir! A precious stone! It cuts into glass as though it were putty.

HOLMES: It is more than a precious stone. It's *the* precious stone.

WATSON: *(screaming)* Not the Countess of Morcar's blue carbuncle?

HOLMES: Precisely so. I have read about it in the newspaper. It is unique and priceless. The reward offered for its return is one thousand pounds, but it is worth far more than that.

PETERSON: *(falling into a chair in disbelief)* A thousand pounds! Great lord of mercy!

WATSON: I believe it was lost at the Hotel Cosmopolitan.

HOLMES: *(shuffling through a pile of newspapers)* Precisely so. Just five days ago. John Horner, a plumber, has been arrested. *(reading from the paper)* It says that James Ryder swore that he had let Horner into the room of the Countess of Morcar in order that he might make a repair. On returning, he found that Horner had disappeared and that the case which held the jewel was empty. They arrested Horner, but could not find the stone.

WATSON: *(taking the newspaper and continuing to read)* Catherine Cusak, maid to the countess, backed up everything that James Ryder had said. Inspector Bradstreet even testified that Ryder had been arrested once before for robbery, and was a likely suspect in this disappearance.

HOLMES: So much for the police! The stone came from the goose and the goose came from Mr. Henry Baker, the gentleman with the bad hat. I will advertise in the paper to find him.

WATSON: What will you say?

HOLMES: *(writing and talking out loud)* "Found at the corner of Goodge Street, a goose and a black felt hat. Mr. Henry Baker can have same by applying at 6:30 this evening at 221B Baker Street."

WATSON: But will he see it?

HOLMES: Sure. He is a poor man and regretted dropping the bird. Also, he will see it because people always notice their own names.

The Substitute Teacher Resource Book • Scholastic Teaching Resources

WATSON: I will put it in all the papers, sir.

HOLMES: Peterson, I will keep the stone for now. Would you please go and buy a goose so that I might have one to give to Mr. Baker when he comes tonight.

SCENE TWO
Later that same evening in Mr. Holmes's suite

HOLMES: Is that your hat, Mr. Baker?

BAKER: Yes, sir. That is undoubtedly my hat. Thank you for returning it to me. And the bird?

HOLMES: We had to eat the bird, lest it would spoil. I have bought you a replacement goose.

BAKER: How very kind of you, sir. Mrs. Baker will be most pleased.

HOLMES: Mr. Baker, would you mind telling me where you got your goose?

BAKER: I got it from Windigate at the Alpha Club. I was a member of the goose club. I paid a little each week until it was mine.

HOLMES: Thank you very much, Mr. Baker.

SCENE THREE
At the Alpha Club

HOLMES: Mr. Windigate. I have just spoken to Mr. Henry Baker who bought a goose from you. Please tell me where you got that same goose.

MR. WINDIGATE: I got them from a salesman named Breckinridge in Covent Garden, but he got them from Mrs. Oakshot who raises them in her backyard.

NARRATOR: But as Holmes and Watson turned to go, a little rat-faced man also came asking about geese.

HOLMES: Excuse me, sir. Are you trying to trace some of Mrs. Oakshot's geese?

STRANGER: (*actually James Ryder*) Oh, sir! If you know something about the location of those geese, you are the very man whom I have longed to meet. I can hardly explain how interested I am in this matter.

HOLMES: Would you happen to be Mr. James Ryder, upper attendant of the Hotel Cosmopolitan? (*The man stares at Holmes in astonishment.*)

SCENE FOUR
221B Baker Street

HOLMES: Now then. You want to know what became of those geese?

RYDER: Oh, yes sir!

HOLMES: Or rather one goose in particular. White with a black bar across the tail?

RYDER: Can you tell me where it is?

HOLMES: Certainly. It came here to me where it laid a remarkable beautiful blue little egg.

NARRATOR: Holmes held up the blue jewel. Ryder jumped to look at the stone in his hand.

HOLMES: The game's up, Ryder. I know it was you who stole the stone from the Countess. I only need one more piece of your ingenious puzzle.

RYDER: Catherine Cusak told me of it.

WATSON: And you knew that Horner had been in trouble for stealing before. He was the perfect person to accuse of this crime.

RYDER: Please have mercy on me. Think of my father and mother! It would break their hearts! I never went wrong before! I will never steal again. Please don't take me to court!

WATSON: But you would have let an innocent man go to jail for your crime!

HOLMES: Let me hear the true account of how the stone came to be in the goose.

RYDER: I stole the stone, but then there was no place to hide it. I went to my sister's house on Brixton Road. Her name is Oakshot. I

The Substitute Teacher Resource Book • Scholastic Teaching Resources

fed it to one of the geese because she had promised me one for Christmas dinner. I thought I would get the stone back then. But when I went to get the goose, she had sold them to a dealer in Covent Garden. Now I am a branded thief without ever having touched the wealth for which I sold my character. Please help me!

(Ryder sobs into his hands.)

HOLMES: Get out!

RYDER: What? Oh, Heaven, bless you!

HOLMES: No more words! Get out of here and I hope you have learned your lesson about stealing.

WATSON: But why did you let him go?

HOLMES: This fellow will not go wrong again. He is too frightened. It is the season for forgiveness. The countess will get back her stone. The commissionaire will get his reward. Mr. Horner will go free as there is no evidence against him. We have had our fun with a whimsical problem of the hat. Ring the bell, Watson, and call for Mrs. Hudson, the cook. Then we will begin another investigation in which a bird will also be the chief feature.

* * * * * * * * * * * * * * * * * * * *

Clue-In Questions for "The Blue Carbuncle"

Sherlock Holmes is famous for his powers of deduction. This means that he could look at the smallest clues and learn important facts about people and about his cases.

Directions: Go back to Scene One to complete this list of facts about Mr. Henry Baker. Opposite each fact, tell *how* Mr. Holmes knew these facts.

Mr. Baker was very smart. _____

Mr. Baker used to have lots of money. _____

Mr. Baker does not have money now. _____

Mr. Baker's wife doesn't care about him. _____

Mr. Baker just had a haircut. _____

Mr. Baker is out of shape and sweats a lot. _____

Mr. Baker uses gas to light his home. _____

Mr. Baker got the goose for his wife. _____

At the end of the play, Sherlock Holmes figured out that James Ryder had taken the stone. Name three clues that helped Mr. Holmes make this deduction.

1. _____

2. _____

3. _____

The Substitute Teacher Resource Book • Scholastic Teaching Resources

Name _____ Date _____

Directions:
Look at the group of shapes
on the right. Using colored
pencils or crayons, trace
the circle in red and
the triangle in blue,
and the rectangle
in yellow.
Then answer the
questions in pencil.

*Remember to show
your work!*

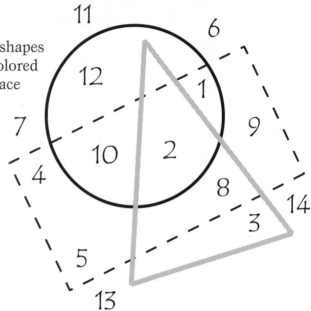

1. What is the sum of the numerals in the circle? _____

2. What is the sum of the numerals in the triangle? _____

3. What is the sum of the numerals in the rectangle? _____

4. Look at the answers to questions number 1, 2, and 3.
Which shape has the largest sum? _____

5. Which shape had the smallest sum? _____

6. What is the difference between
the largest and the smallest sums? _____

7. List all of the numerals that are in the rectangle
but not in any other shape. _____

8. What is the sum of all of the numerals that
are not in any shape? _____

9. List all of the two-digit numerals. _____

10. What is the sum of all of the two-digit numerals? _____

The Substitute Teacher Resource Book • Scholastic Teaching Resources

Name _____ **Date** _____

The third grade at King Elementary School went to visit the science center. They had a wonderful time riding on the bus, viewing the exhibits, and shopping for souvenirs.

Directions: Read the following questions about the field trip and solve the word problems. Remember to show your work in the space next to the problem.

1. On bus number one there were 19 students and 6 adults. How many people were on the bus? _____

2. On bus number two there were more students than adults. There were 24 students and 7 adults. How many more students than adults went on bus number two? _____

3. The bus left school at 9:00 and arrived at the science center at 10:15. How long did it take to travel to the science center? _____

4. Mrs. Smith bought 10 pencils to use in her classroom. Each pencil cost 25 cents. How much money did she spend for the pencils? _____

5. The science center had live animals for students to see. The cobra snake was 47 inches long and the king snake was 33 inches long. How much longer was the cobra than the king snake? _____

The Substitute Teacher Resource Book • Scholastic Teaching Resources

Name _____ **Date** _____

6. The science center had an exhibit about National Champion trees. The tallest tree is the Coast Redwood at 362 feet. The next largest tree is the Coast Douglas-Fir at 298 feet. How much larger is the redwood than the Douglas Fir? _____

7. Students visited the planetarium at the science center. They saw a movie about the planets. It said that Mercury was the smallest planet—only 3,100 miles around. Planet Earth is about 26,000 miles around. How much larger is Earth than Mercury? _____

8. Mark and Tyrell wanted to buy souvenirs. Mark bought a toy turtle for $2.25 and Tyrell got a whistle for $1.50. How much did the boys spend together? _____

9. Jakayla and Brittney were hungry after their tour. Jakayla bought an ice cream cone for $2.50 and Brittney bought a Coke for $1.50. Which girl spent the most money? _____

How much more did she spend than her friend? _____

10. When it was time to go back to school, the bus left the science center at 2:15. What time did they arrive back at school if it took them the same amount of time to travel both directions? _____

The Substitute Teacher Resource Book • Scholastic Teaching Resources

Going on a Field Trip #2

Name _____   **Date** _____

Directions: Read the following questions about the field trip and solve the word problems. Remember to show your work in the space next to the problem.

1. Three buses went to the science center. One bus held 19 students and 6 adults; one had 23 students and 6 adults; and one had 24 students and 7 adults. How many people went to the science center all together? _____

2. How many more students than adults went on the trip? _____

3. The bus left school at 9:15 and arrived at the science center at 10:25. How long did it take to travel to the science center? _____

4. Mrs. Smith bought pencils for each of her students. The pencils cost 25 cents each and she has 25 students. How much money did she spend for the pencils? _____

5. The science center had live animals for students to see. Look at this chart about the snakes:

   cobra   47 inches long

   viper   28 inches long

   asp   31 inches long

   anaconda   63 inches long

   rattlesnake   38 inches long

   What is the total length of all of the snakes together? _____

The Substitute Teacher Resource Book • Scholastic Teaching Resources

Name _____ Date _____

6. The science center had an exhibit about National Champion trees. It said that the largest tree in the United States is the Giant Sequoia. It has a circumference of 83 feet and 2 inches. A foot has 12 inches. How many inches around is the Giant Sequoia? _____

7. Students visited the Planetarium at the science center. They saw a movie about the planets. It said that Mercury was the smallest planet—only 3,100 miles around—and Jupiter was the largest at 88,000 miles in diameter. How much smaller is Mercury than Jupiter? _____

8. Mark and Tyrell wanted to buy souvenirs. Mark bought a toy turtle for $2.25 and a puzzle for $3.15. Tyrell got a whistle for $1.50 and a boat for $3.75. Which boy spent the most money? _____

How much more did he spend than his friend? _____

9. Jakayla was hungry after the tour. Jakayla bought an ice cream cone for $2.40. She gave the clerk $5.00. How much change did she get back? _____

10. When it was time to go back to school, the bus left the science center at 2:15. What time did they arrive back at school if it took them the same amount of time to travel both directions? _____

The Substitute Teacher Resource Book • Scholastic Teaching Resources

Tangram **Puzzler**

Name _____   **Date** _____

Directions: Name the shapes in the large square. These seven basic shapes can be used to make hundreds of designs. Cut out the shapes carefully along the solid lines. First, try to arrange them in a square again. Then try to make the pictures shown below, using all seven shapes.

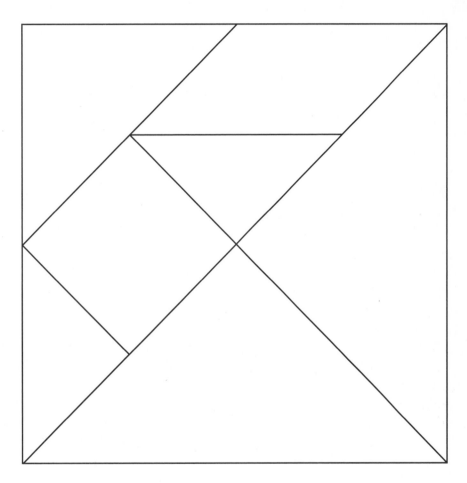

Bonus: On another page, arrange the seven shapes to make your own picture, trace the outline, and let others try to solve it.

The Substitute Teacher Resource Book • Scholastic Teaching Resources

Name _____   **Date** _____

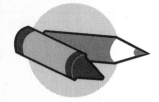

Directions: Get your pencils and crayons ready!
Choose four patterns from the list below and shade in
the boxes on the 100's charts.

Patterns

○ All numbers that contain the digit 6

○ Doubles like 77

○ Count by twos

○ Count by fives

○ Count by threes

○ Count by nines

○ All numbers that are greater than 50

○ All numbers that are less than 50

○ All numbers where the second digit is less than the
first digit. (Example: 94; 4 is less than 9)

○ All numbers where the second digit is greater than
the first digit. (Example: 37; 7 is more than 3)

○ All numbers where the digits add up to 8.
(Example: 71; 7 + 1 = 8)

○ All of the even numbers (in one color) and all of the odd
numbers (another color).

Bonus: *Write your own number pattern here and color it on a 100's chart. See if
others can name the pattern you have colored.*

The Substitute Teacher Resource Book • Scholastic Teaching Resources

100's Chart Number Patterns

Name _____   **Date** _____

1	2	3	4	5	6	7	8	9	10
11	12	13	14	15	16	17	18	19	20
21	22	23	24	25	26	27	28	29	30
31	32	33	34	35	36	37	38	39	40
41	42	43	44	45	46	47	48	49	50
51	52	53	54	55	56	57	58	59	60
61	62	63	64	65	66	67	68	69	70
71	72	73	74	75	76	77	78	79	80
81	82	83	84	85	86	87	88	89	90
91	92	93	94	95	96	97	98	99	100

1	2	3	4	5	6	7	8	9	10
11	12	13	14	15	16	17	18	19	20
21	22	23	24	25	26	27	28	29	30
31	32	33	34	35	36	37	38	39	40
41	42	43	44	45	46	47	48	49	50
51	52	53	54	55	56	57	58	59	60
61	62	63	64	65	66	67	68	69	70
71	72	73	74	75	76	77	78	79	80
81	82	83	84	85	86	87	88	89	90
91	92	93	94	95	96	97	98	99	100

1	2	3	4	5	6	7	8	9	10
11	12	13	14	15	16	17	18	19	20
21	22	23	24	25	26	27	28	29	30
31	32	33	34	35	36	37	38	39	40
41	42	43	44	45	46	47	48	49	50
51	52	53	54	55	56	57	58	59	60
61	62	63	64	65	66	67	68	69	70
71	72	73	74	75	76	77	78	79	80
81	82	83	84	85	86	87	88	89	90
91	92	93	94	95	96	97	98	99	100

1	2	3	4	5	6	7	8	9	10
11	12	13	14	15	16	17	18	19	20
21	22	23	24	25	26	27	28	29	30
31	32	33	34	35	36	37	38	39	40
41	42	43	44	45	46	47	48	49	50
51	52	53	54	55	56	57	58	59	60
61	62	63	64	65	66	67	68	69	70
71	72	73	74	75	76	77	78	79	80
81	82	83	84	85	86	87	88	89	90
91	92	93	94	95	96	97	98	99	100

The Substitute Teacher Resource Book • Scholastic Teaching Resources

Name _____ Date _____

Whales & Dolphins

There are about 76 different kinds of whales and dolphins around the world. Even though they live in water, whales and dolphins are not fish. They are warm-blooded mammals, like cats and dogs and humans. Like other mammals, their babies are born alive and feed on mother's milk. Mammals breathe air and cannot breathe underwater as fish do. Most whales and dolphins must come up for air after several minutes, or they would drown. A few, though, can stay under for an hour or more.

All whales and dolphins belong to the group of mammals called cetaceans. There are two main kinds of cetaceans: those with teeth and those without. Toothed whales have sharp teeth that they use to catch, bite, and kill their prey. Baleen whales, on the other hand, do not have teeth. Instead they have mouths full of hanging plates called *baleen*, which look like big brushes or combs. These are used to filter bits of food from the water. The baleen whales are the real giants of the sea. One kind of baleen whale, the blue whale, is the largest living thing on Earth.

All dolphins are whales, and they have teeth. Names can be confusing, though, especially when some dolphins are called dolphins and some others are called whales. Killer whales, for example, are really dolphins.

The killer whale is one of the handsomest beasts in the sea. It doesn't look much like other dolphins, which are a dull gray or all black. The killer whale is marked with a clear pattern of black and white, and it is the largest of the dolphins. But it is still much smaller than the baleen whales.

Bottlenose dolphins are probably the best-known dolphins. They are the ones most often seen on T.V. and in marine parks. They can be trained to perform jumps, flips, and other exciting moves. Killer whales, too, can be trained to perform jumps and flips. Sea World's Shamu® is one example. During their training and while they are performing, the dolphins are rewarded often, usually with a fish, for carrying out certain behaviors. However, because these are all natural behaviors to begin with, the question is, who's training whom? Dolphins and whales are very intelligent creatures.

The Substitute Teacher Resource Book • Scholastic Teaching Resources

Name _____   **Date** _____

1. The killer whale is really a _____
- ❑ **a.** dolphin.
- ❑ **b.** fish.
- ❑ **c.** porpoise.
- ❑ **d.** baleen whale.

2. Which of these statements is an opinion?
- ❑ **a.** All dolphins are whales.
- ❑ **b.** The killer whale is one of the most handsome beasts in the sea.
- ❑ **c.** Most dolphins are dull gray or all black.
- ❑ **d.** The blue whale is the largest living thing on Earth.

3. What are the two main kinds of cetaceans? Tell how they differ.

_____

_____

_____

_____

_____

4. Whales and dolphins are mammals. What are the characteristics of mammals?

_____

_____

_____

_____

_____

© 2002 by Michael Priestly

The Substitute Teacher Resource Book • Scholastic Teaching Resources

Get the Picture?

Name _____ **Date** _____

Did you know that computer screens are made up of tiny dots called pixels? The computer turns them on or off and changes the color of each tiny dot. What you see is a complete picture.

Directions: Color the dots in the grid as if you are the computer. In order to see the completed scene, have your friend hold the picture up on the other side of the room. You will not believe what is hiding in this ocean scene! For best results, use markers or color darkly with your crayons.

```
2 2 2 2 2 2 2 2 2 2 2 2 2 2 2 2 2 2 2 2 2 4 4 4 4 4 4 4 4 4 4 4 4 4 4 4 4 4 4 4 4 4 4 4
2 2 2 2 2 2 2 2 2 2 2 2 2 2 2 2 2 2 2 2 4 4 4 4 4 5 5 5 5 5 5 4 4 4 4 4 4 5 5 5 5 5 5 5
2 2 2 2 2 2 2 2 2 2 2 2 2 4 4 4 4 5 5 5 5 5 5 5 5 5 5 4 4 4 6 6 6 4 4 5 5 5 5 5
2 2 2 2 2 2 2 2 2 2 2 4 4 4 4 5 5 5 5 5 5 5 5 5 5 5 4 4 4 6 4 6 4 4 4 5 5 5 5
2 2 2 2 2 2 2 2 2 2 4 4 4 4 5 5 5 5 5 5 5 5 5 5 5 5 4 4 4 4 4 4 4 5 5 5 5 5
2 2 2 2 2 2 2 2 4 4 4 4 4 5 5 5 5 5 5 5 5 5 5 5 5 5 5 5 5 5 5 5 5 5 5 5 5 5
2 2 2 2 2 2 2 2 2 2 4 4 4 4 5 5 5 5 5 5 5 5 5 5 5 5 5 5 5 5 5 5 5 5 5 5 5 5
2 2 2 2 2 2 2 2 2 2 2 2 4 4 4 4 5 5 5 5 5 5 5 5 5 5 5 5 5 5 5 5 5 5 5 5 5 5
2 2 2 2 2 2 2 2 2 2 2 2 2 2 4 4 4 4 4 4 4 4 4 5 5 5 5 5 5 5 5 5 5 5 5 5 5 5
2 2 2 2 2 2 2 2 2 2 2 2 2 2 2 2 2 2 2 4 4 4 4 5 5 5 5 5 5 5 5 5 5 5 5 5
2 2 2 2 2 2 2 2 2 2 2 2 2 1 2 2 2 2 2 2 2 2 4 4 5 5 5 5 5 5 5 5 5 5 5 5
2 2 2 2 2 2 1 2 2 1 2 2 1 1 2 2 2 2 2 2 1 2 2 4 4 4 4 4 4 4 4 4 4 4 4 4
2 2 2 2 2 2 1 2 2 1 2 2 1 1 2 2 2 2 2 3 2 2 2 2 6 6 6 6 6 6 6 6 6 4 4 4
2 2 2 2 1 1 2 1 1 1 1 1 2 2 2 2 3 3 3 2 2 6 2 2 6 2 6 6 2 6 6 6 6 4
2 2 2 3 3 3 3 3 3 3 3 3 2 2 2 3 3 3 2 1 2 2 2 2 6 2 2 6 2 6 6 6 2 6 6
2 2 3 3 3 1 1 1 1 1 1 3 2 2 2 3 1 3 1 2 2 2 2 2 6 2 2 2 2 6 2 6 6
2 3 4 3 3 3 3 3 3 3 3 3 2 3 3 3 3 2 2 2 2 2 2 2 2 2 2 2 2 2 6 2
2 3 3 3 1 1 1 1 1 1 1 3 3 3 3 3 1 1 1 3 1 2 2 2 2 2 2 2 2 2 2 2
2 3 3 3 3 3 3 3 3 3 3 3 3 3 3 3 3 2 2 2 2 2 2 2 2 2 2 2 2 2 2
2 3 3 1 1 1 1 1 1 1 3 3 2 2 3 3 1 3 3 1 2 2 2 2 2 2 2 2 2 2 2 6
2 2 3 3 3 3 3 3 3 3 3 2 2 2 3 3 3 1 2 2 2 2 2 2 2 2 2 2 2 6 2 6
2 2 2 1 2 2 1 1 1 2 2 2 1 2 2 2 3 3 2 2 1 2 2 6 2 2 2 2 6 2 2 6 2 6
2 2 2 2 1 2 2 1 1 1 2 2 2 1 2 2 2 3 3 2 2 2 6 2 2 6 2 2 6 2 6 6 6 6
2 2 2 2 2 1 2 2 1 2 2 2 2 2 2 2 3 2 2 2 2 6 6 2 6 2 6 6 2 6 6 6 4
2 2 2 2 2 1 2 2 1 2 2 2 2 2 2 1 2 2 6 6 6 6 6 6 6 6 6 6 6 6 4 4
2 2 2 2 2 2 2 2 2 1 2 2 2 2 2 2 2 4 4 4 4 4 4 4 4 4 4 4 4
2 2 2 2 2 2 2 2 2 2 1 2 2 2 2 2 4 4 4 5 5 5 5 5 5 5 5 5 5 5 5 5
2 2 2 2 2 2 2 2 2 2 1 2 2 2 2 2 4 4 4 5 5 5 5 5 5 5 5 5 5 5 5 4
2 2 2 2 2 2 2 2 2 2 2 2 2 2 2 2 2 4 4 4 4 4 4 4 4 4 4 4 4 4 4
```

Code Key

1	Red	2	Blue	3	Yellow	4	Black	5	Purple	6	White

From *Scholastic's Super Science Blue*, March 1995.

Easy-to-Play Games & Quiet Activities

•

Quick-Take Story

Sequencing, vocabulary, plot development

Write one line of words in a row across the chalkboard (see word box below). Invite students to talk together in small groups of four to six to contrive a fantastic story with a few sentences that include all of these words. Have one member write it down and let a spokesperson for each group read their story out loud. (Note: You may need to model creating a quick-take with students before they begin the task in groups.)

After they have done one or two of these quick-take stories as a group, let students write two on their own. Remind students that these quick-takes are not to be violent, embarrassing to anyone in the room, gross, or classroom inappropriate, but they are supposed to be clever, which means they can be funny, mysterious, factual, or just plain quirky.

You can copy the box below on the board or create a class word box by writing eight general categories on the chalkboard and challenging students to suggest good words for each one. When you have three or four lines from which to choose, allow students to choose the line they want and write their own story. Encourage students who want to write their own words and write their own personal stories to do so. To extend the activity and engage visual learners, ask students to illustrate the sentence or a scene from their story.

NAME	ANIMAL	COLOR	VERB	SOUND	SHAPE OR SIZE	PLACE	GIGGLE WORD
Fred	donkey	purple	stumbled	crash	gigantic	swamp	oops!
Alonzo	spider	green	hurried	whoosh	tiny	bathroom	ouch!
Barbara	whale	red	zoomed	splash	square	car	yikes!
Takema	bear	yellow	groaned	whine	round	swamp	AHHHH!
José	snake	pink	whisked	crinkle	skinny	playground	zowie!

Heads Up, Seven Up

Deduction, social skills

Select seven students to stand in front of the classroom. Have the rest of the students, who are seated at their desks, put their heads down, close their eyes, and extend one hand, closing it into a fist with the thumb sticking up.

Let the seven students sneak quietly around the classroom. Each one will select a seated classmate by gently pushing that student's thumb down on his or her fist. When they have each selected someone and returned to the front of the room, announce "Heads up, seven up." At this time all of the students at their seats raise their heads. The seven who were chosen (by having their thumbs pushed down) stand and take three turns to guess who selected them. If they guess correctly, they get to take a turn as one of the seven selectors. If the guess is incorrect, the selecting student gets another turn.

This simple game is popular even up through the fourth and fifth grades. Don't hesitate to use it, but look out for peekers!

HINT: *When you pick the first round of students, choose one or two students that you think might not be chosen by other students. Even choose the troublemaker. Your smile and kindness might just make that student easier to deal with. Remind students to be sensitive to those who have not yet had a turn.*

Who Stole the . . . ?

Deduction, formulating questions

This game was originally invented to be played at a Valentine's Day party. The name of the game was "Who Stole the Paper Heart?" but as you can see, this simple game can be played with any small object. (Suggestions: Use a flat paper object such as a paper pumpkin, a card, a construction paper turkey feather, a flower, shamrock, large coin, or a fake gift.)

Select a student to be "it." This student sits on a stool in front of the classroom, closes his or her eyes (or is blindfolded), and holds the object that is to be "stolen." Then tiptoe around the classroom and tap the shoulder of the student who will sneak up and gently remove the object from "its" hand. That student returns to his or her seat, puts the object in his desk or sits on it, and tries to look innocent. "It" then gets three chances to guess who stole the heart. Let the student simply read classmates' facial expressions or let him or her ask three yes-or-no questions and then make one guess (e.g., "It" may ask if the thief has hair past her shoulders, is wearing sneakers today, and has a purple barrette). If "it" guesses correctly, the thief has to return the object and "it" gets another turn. If the guess is incorrect, then the thief gets to be "it."

HINT: *You can continue to choose "the thief" to assure that everyone has a turn, or you can allow the retiring "it" to choose the new sneaky thief. Limit the number of turns to two so that each student may have a turn as "it."*

The Whisper Game

Listening, articulating

Have students sit in a row or circle or have older students gather in groups of four to six. Whisper a short poem or nonsense sentence into the ear of one student. He or she must whisper it to the next student, who must whisper it to the student beside him or her, and so on, down the line. The last student has to tell what he or she heard, which is usually drastically different than the original sentence; share the original and let students compare the two versions. Discuss how the whisper game is like a rumor and why it's important always to go to the original source to find out the "real story" if it directly concerns them—and ignore the rumor if it doesn't. Chances are it has changed as it has passed from one speaker to the next and it has become inaccurate.

HINT: *If students are well behaved, you can trust them to think up their own funny sentences for this game. If they are a little rowdy, you should create the sentences or phrases.*

Whisper Game examples:

- Silly Susie swam around swishing for snakes.

- The old crow cawed in the morning, ate in the afternoon, and clawed at night.

- Go down to the store to search for sardines.

- Try turning the top to twist open the twizzle sticks.

- Run 'round the window and wind up the wizard.

Simple Spelling Bee

Spelling, memorization

Using a student's spelling book or the teacher's guide, conduct a spelling bee using words from one of the first units presented. Use only words that you are pretty sure students have studied that year. Follow this format:

All students stand in a line (or half circle) in the room. Start at one end and call out one spelling word to each student. Have the student say the word, spell it, and say the word again. If the word is spelled correctly, go to the next student and present a new word. If the word is missed, that same word is given to the next student. No one sits down or is "out" of the game.

HINTS:

- *If students have a difficult time behaving during the spelling bee, switch to a paper bee. Have students use a standard sheet of notebook paper. Instruct them to fold it in half five times so that when it is unfolded it will be a grid of 32 boxes. Each time you give out a word, the student writes it in a different box. You can give 32 or 64 words. The papers can be scored individually or the total number of correct responses can be added to get a team score.*

- *If you give prizes for this game, try giving them to anyone who scores above a certain number correct. For example, if you use 64 words, give a prize to any student who spells more than 54 correctly.*

- *Stickers from your tote bag make great prizes. If you are out of these, write "GREAT SPELLER" on a stick-on name tag and give these to students to wear to lunch or home to show their families.*

Favorite Activities **T**racking Chart

As you travel from classroom to classroom, you may find it difficult to remember which activities you have used with particular groups. Keep track of your favorite activities (and add ideas for modifications) by filling in this chart after you complete each assignment.

Activity	Date/ School	Grade/ Class	Comments *(e.g., level of difficulty, how students responded, how to model, ways to group students, time allotment, and so on.)*

Favorite Activities Tracking Chart

Activity	Date/ School	Grade/ Class	Comments *(e.g., level of difficulty, how students responded, how to model, ways to group students, time allotment, and so on.)*

Pages 58–59, Match It! States and Capitals
1. (J) Sacramento, California 2. (EE) Columbus, Ohio 3. (B) Charleston, West Virginia 4. (N) Montpelier, Vermont 5. (NN) Topeka, Kansas 6. (H) Phoenix, Arizona 7. (BB) Austin, Texas 8. (X) Albany, New York 9. (XX) Carson City, Nevada 10. (C) Santa Fe, New Mexico 11. (A) Nashville, Tennessee 12. (CC) Baton Rouge, Louisiana 13. (UU) Trenton, New Jersey 14. (G) Juneau, Alaska 15. (DD) Hartford, Connecticut 16. (PP) Honolulu, Hawaii 17. (HH) Frankfort, Kentucky 18. (II) Boston, Massachusetts 19. (S) Helena, Montana 20. (VV) Lincoln, Nebraska 21. (KK) Salem, Oregon 22. (LL) Columbia, South Carolina 23. (MM) Harrisburg, Pennsylvania 24. (XX) Concord, New Hampshire 25. (AA) Madison, Wisconsin 26. (R) Olympia, Washington 27. (SS) Salt Lake City, Utah 28. (U) Atlanta, Georgia 29. (Y) Jackson, Mississippi 30. (V) Lansing, Michigan 31. (E) Annapolis, Maryland 32. (L) Augusta, Maine 33. (GG) Des Moines, Iowa 34. (D) Springfield, Illinois 35. (OO) Indianapolis, Indiana 36. (FF) Tallahassee, Florida 37. (UU) Dover, Delaware 38. (K) Denver, Colorado 39. (I) Little Rock, Arkansas 40. (F) Montgomery, Alabama 41. (Q) Cheyenne, Wyoming 42. (P) Richmond, Virginia 43. (O) Pierre, South Dakota 44. (T) St. Paul, Minnesota 45. (Z) Raleigh, North Carolina 46. (RR) Bismarck, North Dakota 47. (QQ) Boise, Idaho 48. (M) Oklahoma City, Oklahoma 49. (JJ) Providence, Rhode Island 50. (W) Jefferson City, Missouri

Page 60, Match It! Who Wrote Which Book?
1. *The Tale of Peter Rabbit*, Beatrix Potter 2. *The Cat in the Hat*, Dr. Seuss 3. *Where the Sidewalk Ends*, Shel Silverstein 4. *Winnie the Pooh*, A. A. Milne 5. *Harry Potter and the Sorcerer's Stone*, J. K. Rowling 6. *Charlotte's Web*, E. B. White 7. *Tales of a Fourth Grade Nothing*, Judy Blume 8. *Little House on the Prairie*, Laura Ingalls Wilder 9. *Freckle Juice*, Judy Blume 10. *Brown Bear, Brown Bear*, Eric Carle 11. *Caps for Sale*, Esphyr Slobodkina 12. *Where the Wild Things Are*, Maurice Sendak 13. *Miss Nelson Is Missing*, James Marshall 14. *The Snowy Day*, Ezra Jack Keats 15. *Swimmy*, Leo Lionni 16. *500 Hats of Bartholomew Cubbins*, Dr. Seuss 17. *The Boxcar Children*, Gertrude Chandler Warner 18. *Strega Nona*, Tomie de Paola 19. *Curious George*, H. A. Rey 20. *Sarah Plain and Tall*, Patricia MacLachlan

Page 61, Match It! President Who?
1. John Fitzgerald Kennedy 2. Franklin Delano Roosevelt 3. John Quincy Adams 4. Millard Fillmore 5. Rutherford Brichard Hayes 6. Grover Cleveland 7. James Knox Polk 8. Lyndon Baines Johnson 9. Ulysses Simpson Grant 10. Calvin Coolidge 11. Herbert Hoover 12. Gerald Rudolph Ford 13. James Abram Garfield 14. Richard Milhouse Nixon 15. James Earl Carter

Page 62, Match It! What's the Name of the Group?
1. a flock of pigeons 2. a bed of oysters (or clams) 3. a colony of ants 4. a leap of leopards 5. a plague of locusts 6. a pride of lions 7. a school of fish 8. a swarm of bees 9. a troop of monkeys 10. a murder of crows 11. a pod of whales (or seals) 12. a clowder of kittens 13. a covey of quail 14. a knot of frogs 15. a rafter of turkeys 16. a gaggle of geese 17. a crash of rhinoceros 18. a parliament of owls

Page 63, Idioms—The Spice of Our Language
Answers will vary.
1. He cannot sit still. 2. He is not moving. 3. Don't tell the secret. 4. Four-leaf clovers are very rare. 5. Now he will change his ways. 6. The boy was very happy. 7. It was raining very hard. 8. That noise makes me crazy. 9. She was faking her crying. 10. There is no reason to cry over things that have already happened when you can't change them. 11. You are looking for an answer in the wrong place. 12. He was unable to talk. 13. I can't think of anything else to do. 14. He can't hit anything at all. 15. The shoes were very expensive.

Page 64, Idiom Crossword Fun: Clothes
Across: 1. pants 2. bonnet 3. collar 4. pajama 6. vest 7. cap 9. shoestring 11. apron *Down:* 1. pocket 2. britches 5. jacket 8. coat 10. glove

Page 65, Idiom Crossword Fun: Animals
Across: 1. frog 3. rat 5. weasel 8. wolf 10. skunk 12. chicken 14. snake *Down:* 2. rat 4. clam 6. sponge 7. monkey 9. hound 11. duck 13. horse

Page 66, Idiom Crossword Fun: Food
Across: 2. candy 4. bacon 8. beans 10. nut 11. cake 12. potato 13. apple 14. molasses *Down:* 1. bananas 3. hotcakes 5. fruitcake 6. pancake 7. pickle 8. beans 9. sardines

Page 67, Crack the Code
easy, seed he, eve he, ache a (lot), deed he, eke a, icy, be a, help he, lazy, seek a, any

Page 68, Mother Goose Rhyme Time
dog, bare, dog, dish, cat, jig, flute, coat, shoes, clothes, wow.

Page 69, Limerick Fun *(Students' limericks will vary.)*

Page 70, The Case of the Frog Prince
writing, disappointed, refused, turn, apologized, again, comment, enough, very, wrecking, terrible, although, delicious, palace, afraid, college, doubt, reconsider, where, right

Page 71, The Case of the Terrible Tooth Fairy
received, kitchen, whipped, sandwich, Afterwards, dancing, screaming, nearly, heard, quietly, carefully, believe, problem, another, understand

Pages 72–73, Persuade Me
(Answers will vary. Following are some examples of appropriate answers.) 1. Anson Wong made his living smuggling illegal animals. 2. Smuggling animals is cruel to the animals because they are not in proper containers with food and water and a place to move about. Many animals die during the smuggling. 3. Animal smuggling is bad for planet Earth because many of the smuggled animals are endangered. It upsets the balance of our planet when even one species is lost. 4. Mr. Wong was successful because he was hard to catch and many people will pay large amounts of money for rare and unusual pets. 5. The author is trying to persuade the reader not to purchase exotic pets that may have been shipped to this country illegally. Other answers may include: The author says not to buy animals that are endangered. The author says not to buy animals that are not here legally. The author says not to buy animals from someone who is not in the legal pet business.

Pages 76–79, "The Blue Carbuncle"
Mr. Baker was smart because he had a large head; he used to have lots of money because he had an expensive hat; he has lost his money because he needs a new hat and hasn't purchased one; his wife doesn't care about him because she has not cleaned or brushed his hat for him; there were small hairs like clippings left just after a haircut. Mr. Baker is heavy, so it causes him to perspire a lot; there are no candle-wax stains, so he uses gas to light his home; the tag on the goose said, "For Mrs. Henry Baker." *Key clues are* 1. Ryder was at the scene of the crime. 2. He knew Catherine Cusak. 3. He was nervous and anxious to find out about the goose.

Page 80, Intersecting Shapes and Numbers
1. 25 2. 13 3. 39 4. the rectangle 5. the triangle 6. 26 7. 4, 5, 9 8. 51 9. 10, 11, 13, 14 10. 48

Page 81, Going on a Field Trip #1
1. 25 people 2. 17 3. one hour and fifteen minutes or 75 minutes 4. $2.50 5. 14 inches 6. 64 feet 7. 22,900 miles 8. $3.75 9. Jakayla spent more money. She spent one dollar more than Brittney. 10. 3:30

Page 83, Going on a Field Trip #2
1. 85 people 2. 66 more 3. One hour and ten minutes or 70 minutes 4. $6.25 5. 207 inches 6. 998 inches 7. 84,900 miles 8. Mark spent the most money. He spent 15 cents more than Tyrell. 9. $2.60 10. 3:25.

Page 85, Tangram Puzzler

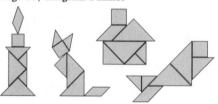

Page 87, 100's Chart
Numbers that contain the digit 6: 6, 26, 36, 46, 56, 66, 76, 86, 96
Doubles: 11, 22, 33, 44, 55, 66, 77, 88, 99
Count by twos: 2, 4, 6, 8, 10....100
Count by fives: 5, 10, 15, 20...100
Count by threes: 3, 6, 9, 12, 15...99
Count by nines: 9, 18, 27, 36...99
Numbers greater than 50: 51–100
Numbers less than 50: 1–49
Numbers in which the second digit is less than the first: 10, 20, 21, 30, 31, 32, 40, 41, 42, 43, 50, 51, 52, 53, 54, 60, 61, 62, 63, 64, 65, 70, 71, 72, 73, 74, 75, 76, 80, 81, 82, 83, 84, 85, 86, 87, 90, 91, 92, 93, 94, 95, 96, 97, 98, 100
Numbers in which the second digit is greater than the first: 12, 13, 14, 15, 16, 17, 18, 19, 23, 24, 25, 26, 27, 28, 29, 34, 35, 36, 37, 38, 39, 45, 46, 47, 48, 49, 56, 57, 58, 59, 67, 68, 69, 78, 79, 89
Odd numbers: 1, 3, 5, 7...99
Even numbers: 2, 4, 6, 8...100

Page 89, Whales and Dolphins
1. A 2. B 3. Toothed whales and baleen whales. The toothed whales have teeth. The baleen whales do not; instead they have large hanging plates called *baleen*. 4. Mammals are born alive, breathe air, and drink milk from their mothers.

Page 91, Get the Picture?
Picture should reveal a shark.